The European Menu Guide

A.

First published in Great Britain in 2002 by
Absolute Press
Scarborough House
29 James Street West
Bath BA1 2BT
England
Phone 44 (0) 1225 316013
Fax 44 (0) 1225 445836
E-mail info@absolutepress.demon.co.uk
Website www.absolutepress.demon.co.uk

A catalogue record of this book is available from
the British Library

ISBN 1 899791 78 7

Printed and bound in Great Britian by
The Cromwell Press

Editors:
Sarah Jane Evans
Gil Rowley

Contents

Introduction

If you're tripping up over *brandades* and *brioche* in France or *strudels* and *Sauerkraut* in Germany, this book is for you. If you're wondering what you dare sprinkle over your *bucatini*, *fettucine* or *tagliolini* whilst in Italy or bidding the *camarones* instead of the *camarero* in Spain, then this book is for you, too. Beads of sweat have been known to flower on foreheads of even the most seasoned travellers as they try to fathom the complexities of the European menu and crash embarrassingly between fluked and failed interpretation.

Fear not! This book unlocks the mysteries of the menus of Europe's four major cuisines. It provides exhaustive listings and explanations of the dishes that the traveller is most likely to find in his quest for an authentic taste of what each country has to offer. It includes a wide variety of classical, regional and modern dishes, and a selection of restaurant terms (so that you can ask the *camarero* for the bill – and dive despairingly towards the *salida* when it arrives).

The European Menu Guide is an essential companion for anyone travelling abroad who enjoys good food and eating out. Don't set foot in *trattoria* or *ristorante* without it.

France

The cuisine of the French is not one cuisine but many. There is the traditional haute cuisine of the grand restaurants and hotels, with its rich sauces and lavish use of expensive ingredients such as butter, cream, truffles, wines and spirits. There is French home cooking – perhaps heartier, certainly less rich, but still executed with the utmost care (even at family level, cooking and eating are regarded respectively as an art and great joy of life). Then there is the upstart newcomer, nouvelle cuisine, which proved that superb dishes can be created without the use of cholesterol-laden ingredients and extolled the virtues of exquisite presentation over quantity. The Japanese have always known this, of course, but the French hailed the discovery as their own and put their own Gallic stamp on it.

Yet this is not all: France is many regions, each with its own individual character and its own specialities. You will eat a very different type of meal in Alsace from the type you would eat on the Provençal coast and that would be quite different again from the food of Bourgogne or of Brittany. You will also find foreign influences – France's associations with North Africa have made *couscous* widely popular and you will find *paella* and *pizza*, to say nothing of the ubiquitous hamburger restaurants, throughout the country.

There is much to explore in this land of 'foodies', and wherever you eat in France you will benefit from the fact that the French are very discerning restaurant customers. You will also see, particularly at lunchtime on Sundays, whole families, often three generations, out enjoying their favourite *biftek* with mountains of *frites* and a steady flow of red wine.

While you are in France, have a wander round the food-stores as well as eating in the restaurants. It will tell you a lot about French food and will also help you to find your way around the restaurant menus.

Phrases For The Restaurant

I want to reserve a table for..... at .....
Je voudrais réserver une table pour.....à .....

Have you a table for.....
Avez-vous une table pour.....

A quiet table
Une table dans un coin tranquil, s'il vous plaît

A table near the window
Une table près de la fenêtre

A table on the terrace
Une table sur la terrasse

Could we have another table please?
Nous voudrions changer de table, s'il vous plaît?

I am in a hurry/ we are in a hurry
Je suis pressé/Nous sommes pressés

Please bring me the menu
Apportez-moi le menu, s'il vous plaît

Can we have a .... please
Nous boulons un ..... s'il vous plaît

Local dishes
Plats régionaux

How much is it?
Combien ça coûte?

What is it?
Qu'est-ce que c'est que ça?

I did not order this
Ce n'est pas ça que j'ai commandé

Too much
C'est trop, Un peu plus

The bill please
L'addition, s'il vous plaît

Is service included?
Est-ce que le service est compris?

I think there is a mistake in the bill
Je pense qu'il y a une erreure dans l'addition

Do you accept travellers' cheques?
Acceptez-vous les chèques de voyage?

Restaurant Terms

addition
  bill
apéritif
  drink taken before the meal (to stimulate the appetite)
bistro, bistrot
  café, small restaurant
brasserie
  restaurant serving meals, snacks and drinks, usually from
  early morning to late at night
carte
  menu; à la, choice of entire menu
commande, sur
  ('on request'), cooked to order
compris
  included
couvert
  cover (charge)
crêperie
  restaurant serving mainly crêpes
déjeuner
  lunch
dessert
  dessert
dîner
  dinner
entrée
  main course
garçon, monsieur
  waiter
hors d'oeuvre
  appetizer, starter
menu
  fixed-price menu, as apposed to à la carte
pichet
  flask for wine
plat du jour
  dish of the day

European Menu Guide

prix fixe
   set price (menu)
petit déjeuner
   breakfast
restaurant
   restaurant
service compris
   service included
souper
   supper
table
   table; d'hôte (host's table), fixed-price menu of several
   courses
verre
   glass

Menu Terms

abats offal

abricot apricot

agneau lamb; *de lait*, baby; *pascal* (Easter), spring

aigre sour, bitter

aigre-doux sweet and sour

aiguillette sliver, particularly from the breast (poultry or game); also top part of rump (beef)

aiglefin haddock

ail garlic

aile wing (on poultry)

aileron tip of the wing (on poultry)

aïllade pertaining to a dish made with garlic; also a garlic mayonnaise, with tomatoes and herbs

aïoli, ailloli type of mayonnaise containing a good deal of garlic (also, optionally, breadcrumbs); in the Midi, complete dish with cod, snails and vegetables

air, enl´ puffed, puffs

Albert creamy horseradish sauce

Albertine sauce from fish made with white wine, mushrooms and truffles

albigeoise, à l´ in the style of Albi, in the Languedoc, with stuffed tomatoes, ham and potatoes

Albuféra see *caneton*

allumettes 'matchsticks', very thin-cut potatoes or pastry puffs

alose shad, speciality of the Gironde, often grilled; sometimes stuffed with sorrel

alsacienne, à l´ Alsace-style, often indicating the presence of pickled cabbage (*choucroute*) and/or *foie gras*; or potatoes; or sausage; otherwise maderia sauce, truffles, noodles and *foie gras*

amande almond

amandin(e) almond-flavoured

américaine American; see also *armoricaine*

ananas pineapple

anchois anchovy

andouilles black-skinned sausages made from port tripe,

served cold

andouillettes sausage made from pork intestine, served hot with mustard

anglaise, a l´ in the English style; various meanings, e.g. served plain, or boiled, or (of fish) dipped in beaten eggs and coated in breadcrumbs

anguille eel; *aux pruneaux*, sautéed, cooked in wine, with prunes (speciality of Brittany and the Pays Nantais); *au vert*, with white wine and green herbs, served cold (speciality of Lille)

ardennaise, à l´ Ardennes-style, with juniper berries

argenteuil soup (*crème*) or other dish containing asparagus

Armagnac brandy, from Gascony, similar in style and quality to Cognac

armoricaine, à l´ (sometimes, incorrectly, *américaine*) Breton-style (Armorica is Brittany); sauce, especially for lobster, containing white wine, cognac, tomatoes and butter

artichauts globe artichokes; *à la bretonne* (Brittany-style), with cider and onions; favorite, with asparagus and cheese; *fonds d´*, bottoms

asperges asparagus; *à la flamande* (Flanders-style), with a butter and egg-yolk sauce

assiette anglaise

('English plate'), dish of assorted cold meats, perhaps with gherkins to garnish, served as an appetizer

assorti mixed, assorted

aubergine aubergine

Aurore velouté sauce with tomato (named after his mother by Brillat-Savarin)

auvergnate, à l´ Auvergne-style, often denoting the presence of cabbage

avocat avocado; *vinaigrette*, with vinaigrette

avoine oat

baba au rhum sponge cake soaked in rum (rum baba)

baguette long, thin loaf of white bread

baie berry

ballotine boned and rolled meat, poultry, fish or game, similar to a *galatine* but served hot (occasionally cold) as a main course

Banon refreshing, slightly sharp-tasting cow's-milk cheese (sometimes made with goat and sheep milk, and sometimes marinated in *marc*), made in Provence

barbue brill

basquaise, à la Basque-style, with tomatoes and peppers, and often rice; garnished with *cèpes*, Bayonne ham and potatoes

bâtarde thick butter sauce flavoured with lemon

bavarois, crème bavaroise moulded egg yolks and whipped cream, served cold as a dessert with fruit or chocolate

bayonnaise, à la Bayonne-style, with Bayonne ham

béarnaise classic sauce made with egg yolks, vinegar and herbs, thickened with butter

Beaucaire see *carré*

Beaufort fruity cow's-milk cheese if gruyère/Emmental type, made in the Beaufort mountains (Savoie)

bécasse woodcock

béchamel basic white sauce made with flour, butter and milk

beignet small sweet or savoury fritter

belle dijonnaise, à la (in the style of the beauty from Dijon), dessert wih blackcurrants

Bercy (name denotes Paris origin), sauce for fish, made with shallots, white wine and butter

betterave beetroot

beurre butter; *ail*, garlic; *anchois*, with anchovy; *blanc*, sauce for fish, made with shallots cooked in white wine and vinegar, with butter whipped in; *breton*, with herbs; *d'escargots* ('snail'), seasoned butter with shallots, parsley and garlic; *maître d'hôtel* ('head waiter's'), with parsley; *marchand de vin* ('wine-merchant's'), with shallots and red wine; *de Montpellier*, with herbs, eggs, garlic and anchovies; *noir* ('black'), browned with vinegar and capers; *noix*, walnut; *noisette* ('hazelnut'), lightly browned

beurre de Gascogne Pork dripping with garlic

bière beef; *bouteille*, bottled; *pression*, draught

bien cuit well cooked (of steak)

bifteck steak (usually beef, sometimes hores), for frying or grilling; see also *saignant*, *à point*, *bleu*, *bien cuit*, *tartare*

European Menu Guide

bigarade orange sauce, often served with duck or game

biscuit sponge cake

bisque thick fish soup (especially of lobster, also crayfish, etc.) with white wine and cream

blanc white

blanchaille whitebait

blanquette casserole, often of veal, with onions, mushrooms and cream sauce

blé wheat, corn; *noir*, buckwheat

bleu blue (of cheese); nearly raw (of steak); poached with vinegar (of trout)

Bleu d'Auvergne cow's-milk version of Roquefort with a rich, sharp, salty and rich, made in thr Auvergne

Bleu de Bresse creamy blue cow's milk cheese made in the Jura region

Bleu des Causses cow's-milk cheese of roquefort type, sharp, salty and rich, made in Aquitaine

boeuf beef; *bourguignon* or *(à la) bourguignonne* (Burgundy-style), in red wine, with mushrooms, onions and bacon; *en daube*, stewed in red wine with bacon, salt pork and vegetables; *à la mode*, cooked in wine with vegetables and herbs, served either cold in jelly *(en gelée)* or hot

bohémienne (Bohemian style), garnish of rice flavoured with tomatoes and fried sliced onion; cold béchamel sauce with egg yolks and vinegar

bombe (glacée) ice-cream made in a special mould, often incorporating more than one flavour

Bondon unripened Neufchâtel-type cheese with a fresh, slightly salty flavour and vey little aroma, made in Normandy

bonne-femme ('good wife'), with white wine, mushrooms and onions (especially sole, also poultry)

bordelaise (in the style of Bordeaux, or of the Bordelais), sauce of shallots, (red) wine and tarragon; garnish of artichokes and potatoes, or of *cèpes*, parsley, shallots and potatoes

borscht soup of Russian origin, made with beetroot and served with soured cream

bouchée mouthful; small pastry (with savoury filling)

boudin large sausage; *blanc*, white sausages; *noir*, black pudding; *de Poitou*, with cream, eggs, milk, bread and spinach; *de Strasbourg*, smoked sausage made with pork, onion and bread (from Alsace region)

bouillabaisse classic fish stew of Mediterranean coast (Provence) made with various fish and shell fish, olive oil, garlic, tomatoes and saffron

bouilleture, bouilliture stew; *d'anguilles*, baby eels cooked in white wine with garlic, onion and egg yolkd (speciality of the Poitevin marshes area)

bouillon broth, stock, soup

boulangère (baker's style), baked, with onions and potatoes

bouquet garni bunch of herbs (e.g. parsley, bay and thyme) used to flavour soups and stews

bouquetière (flower-girl's-style), artichokes, carrots, turnips, green beans, peas and cauliflower florets

bourdaloue poached fruit in thick cream with a coating of vanilla custard and crushed macaroons, served hot; *tarte*, pear tart with custard

bourdelot pastry encasing whole apples (speciality of Normandy)

bourguigononne see *boeuf*

bourride Provençal fish soup with *aïoli* (garlic mayonnaise)

Boursalut aromatic, mild but rich-flavoured cow's milk cheese made in the Ile-de-France and Normandy

Boursin rich, creamy cow's milk cheese, sometimes rolled in black pepper or mixed with garlic and parsley

brandade de morue salt cod in a purée made with oil and milk, seasoned with garlic, sometimes with truffles (speciality of Languedoc)

brebis ewe

brème bream; *farcie*, stuffed

bretonne *velouté* sauce with vegetables served with poultry or fish

Briand see *chevreuil*

Brie smooth, butter-textured, white cow's-milk cheese, with a full, mellow flavour, made in the Ile-de-France, Champagne, Burgundy and Lorraine; *de Coulommiers*, cream-enriched version; *de Meaux*, matured version

brioche bun made from rich egg dough, sometimes

containing savoury filling

brochet pike

brochette skewer; meat or fish pieces, or other food, cooked on a skewer

brocoli broccoli

brûlé(e) burnt

bruxelloise, à la Brussels-style; with brussels sprouts and chicory in butter; with hard-boiled yolk of egg in butter, *potage*, brussels-sprouts soup

bûche 'log', rolled sponge cake; *de Noël*, a specila Christmas version

cabassol lamb tripe (speciality of Lanuedoc)

cabillaud fresh cod

café (black) coffee; *complet*, Continental breakfast, *crème*, white; *grande crème*, large breakfast-cup of white coffee; *express*, espresso

caille quail; *à la vigneronne* (wine-grower-style), with grapes and *marc* (speciality of Burgundy)

Camembert mild, creamy cow's-milk cheese made in Normandy

canapés cocktail snacks; *à la bayonnaise* (Bayonne-style), pieces of bread topped with herb butter and Bayonne ham

canard duck; *pressé*, pressed (suffocated), roasted, with the blood and juices served as a sauce (speciality of Rouen); *sauvage*, wild (e.g. mallard). See also *caneton*

cancalaise, à la in the style of Cancale in Brittany (usually, with oysters)

caneton duckling; *d'Albuféra*, with Bayonne ham, mushrooms and madeira sauce; *à la bigarade* (or *à l'orange*), with orange sauce; *au Muscadet*, roast, with a sauce of Muscadet, shallots and cream (specilaity of the Pays Nantais). See also *canard*

Cantal, (fourme de) yellow, Cheddar-like cow's milk cheese from the Auvergne (that labelled *'haute montagne'* has the best flavour)

câpres capers

caprice des Dieux small, oval-shaped, creamy cow's milk cheese, like an enriched Brie, made in the Champagne region

carbonnade grill or braise, theoretically over charcoal; *de* *boeuf* (*à la flamande*), lean beef (Flemish style), sautéed, braised with onions and beet; *de porc*, charcoal-grilled pork slices

cari curry

carottes carrots; *Vichy*, boiled and tossed in butter and parsley

carpe carp; *à la bière*, cooked in beer, with soft roe; *farcie à l'alsacienne*, cooked in white wine, stuffed with other creamed fish, served in white wine, stuffed with other creamed fish, served with pickled cabbage and potatoes (Alsatian version of *gefüllte Fisch*); *à la juive* (Jewish style), boned, cut into sections and served cold with a sauce

carré ('square'), best end of neck (often of lamb or mutton), rack; *d'agneau Beaucaire*, roast lamb with artichokes; *de porc à la limousine* (Limousin-style), roast pork with braised cabbage and chestnuts

Carré de l'Est white-rinded cow's-milk cheese, like a softer and milder Camembert, made in the Champagne region

cassis blackcurrant; (*crème de*), blackcurrant liqueur

cassoulet casserole of haricot beans, tomatoes, garlic and different kinds of meat, especially *confit d'oie*, pork and mutton (speciality of Languedoc)

cayenne type of pepper

céleri celery; also abbreviated form of *céleri-rave*

céleri-rave celeriac

cendré (cindered'), cured in ashes: generic name for goat cheeses so treated

cèpes boletus mushrooms; *à la bordelaise* (Bordelais-style), sautéed, with shallots and parsley

cerfeuil chervil

cerise cherry

cerneaux green walnuts; *aux verjus*, marinated in grape juice, sprinkled with chervil (appetizer, speciality of Touraine)

cervelas saveloy, pork sausage, oftern including pistachios and truffles; *de Lyon*, or *en brioche*, baked inside a brioche crust

cervelles brains; usually calf's, occasionally pig's

Chabichou conical goat's-milk cheese with full flavour and strong animal smell, made in the Poitou region

champignon mushroom

chanterelle small yellow mushroom shaped like a trumpet

Chantilly see *crème*; also type of mayonnaise or white
sauce with lemon juice and whipped cream added

charcuterie an hors d'oeuvre of, strictly speaking, pork
products, but often covers all sorts of meat productions

charcutière (pork-butcher's style), sauce forpork, made
with onions, white wine, winegar, mustard and gherkins

charlotte mould for desserts; hot pudding with fruit inside a
bread-lined mould; (*russe*), sponge fingers with cream or
mousse and sometimes fruit

chasseur hunter's style; garnished with mushrooms, shallots
and parsley; *consommé*, game soup with port garnished
with mushrooms shreds; sauce with shallots, white wine,
tomato and mushrooms

châtaigne chestnut; *d'eau*, water

Châteaubriand grilled porterhouse steak (usually for two)
with a rich sauce of wine, tarragon and shallots, served
with *pommes château*

châtelaine, à la (Lady-of-the-manor style), garnish of which
several versions exist, e.g. with artichoke bottoms, onion
purée, madeira sauce, chestnuts, and sometimes also very
small potatoes

chaude large fruit tart (speciality of Lorraine)

chaud-froid ('hot-cold'), cold velouté sauce, for meat or
poultry, made with aspic jelly, egg yolk and cream

chaudrée fish soup of the Poitou region made with sole,
plaice, eel and white wine, similar to *bouillabaisse*

chausson turnover, made with puff pastry and usually
containing a savoury filling

cheval horse

chèvre generic name for goat's cheese; *blanc*, firm, crumbly
and sweet; *cendré*, cured in cinders to stop mould and
hence with blackened outsides

chevreau kid

chevreuil venison, usually roe deer; *en*, cooked like
venison; *sauce*, sauce for game made with vegetable stock
and red wine (also, potionally, redcurrant jelly); *selle de
Briand*, saddle of, roasted, with pears in red wine

chevrotin name for various goat's-milk cheeses

chicorée endive; *frisée*, curly endive

chiffonade (1) dressing for salad made with vinaigrette, beetroot, hard-boiled eggs and parsley: (2) leaf vegetables cooked with butter and served in a cream sauce

Chivry velouté sauce or butter made with white wine, chervil, parsley, tarragon and chives, and shallots

chocolat chocolate; cup of

choron béarnaise sauce with tomato; garnish of artichokes

chou cabbage; *cabus*, white; *farci*, stuffed; *vert*, green

choucroute pickled cabbage, *sauerkraut* (speciality of Alsace); *à la strasbourgeoise* (Strasbourg-style), with pork, Strasbourg sausages and probably also thin-sliced ham

chouée boiled, buttered cabbage of the Vendée, usually served with potatoes

chou-fleur cauliflower; *à la polonaise* (Polish-style), boiled, coated with breadcrumbs and hard-boiled egg and fried

chou-navet swede

chou-rave kohl rabi

chou-rouge red cabbage

choux choux pastry (*pâte à chou*, type of puff pastry); *au fromage*, cheese puffs

choux brocolis broccoli

choux de Bruxelles brussels sprouts

choux de Chine Chinese cabbage, Chinese leaves

ciboule spring onion

ciboulette chives

cidre cider (speciality of Normandy and Brittany)

cigarette (russe) cigarette-shaped biscuit

citron lemon; *pressé*, fresh, squeezed juice, served as a drink with sugar

civet rich stew; *de lièvre*, hare, casseroled with red wine and onions

clafouti(s) flan or pancake with fruit, especially cherries

Clamart pea soup; *à la*, garnish of peas and artichoke hearts

clou de girofle clove

cochon pig; *de lait*, suckling

cocotte small ovenproof dish, especially for *oeufs en cocotte*, baked eggs (often with cream) in individual dishes; *en*, general description denoting casserole (cooked in casserole

European Menu Guide

dish)

cognac brandy, especially from the Charentes region

coeur heart; *de boeuf, de veau,* calf's; *à la crème,* small heart-shaped cow's-milk cheese, eaten with fresh fruit, or sugar, and cream; *de filet,* finest part of beef fillet

coeurs de palmier palm hearts; palm-tree shoots served hot or cold with viniagrette as an appetizer

coing quince

Colbert see *huîtres*

colin hake; *à la grenobloise* (Grenoble-style), cooked in butter with capers and lemon

compote poached fresh or dried fruit served (usually cold) in its own syrup

Comté gruyère-style cow's-milk cheese with large holes, like a stronger, fruitier Emmental; made in the Franche-Comté

concassé crushed, chopped up or ground

concombre cucumber

condé, (a la) cooked fruit on rice pudding, moistened with fruit syrup

confit (1) goose (*d'oie*), duck, turkey, pork or other meat cooked and sealed in its own fat: (2) preserved fruit (crystallized or condied)

confiture jam

conserve preserve of any kind, including canned meat, vegetables or fish

consommations café fare (drinks, snacks)

consommé clear soup; *en gelée,* served cold

coppa Corsican smoked pork sausage

coq cock (in practice, usually a hen); *au vin,* in red wine, with mushrooms, bacon and garlic; *au vin jaune,* in white wine (yellow Arbois wine), thickened with cream and served with *morilles* (speciality of the Franche-Comté)

coquillages shellfish

coquilles scallop shells

coquilles St Jacques scallops; *à la bretonne* (Breton-style), topped with breadcrumbs and baked; *flambées,* cooked in white wine, with sautéed mushrooms, flamed with cognac and finished with cream; *au vermouth,* cooked in vermouth, white wine, cream and mushrooms

cordon bleu/rouge (blue/red ribbon), denoting high degree of culinary skill; describing veal (*bleu*), escalope wrapped round cheese and ham; describing steak (*tournedos cordon rouge*), with ham and *foie gras*, served in a cognac sauce

cornichon gherkin

côte (1) rib (e.g. *de boeuf*, beef): (2) chop; *de porc à l'alsacienne* (Alsace-style), pork, served with sauerkraut, Strasbourg sausages and boiled potatoes; *de porc à la bayonnaise* (Bayonne-style), marinated pork, with cèpes and new potatoes; *de porc à la gasconne* (Gascony-style), marinated, served with a sauce of olives, garlic, white wine and parsley; *de porc à la vosgienne* (Vosges-style), pork, served with onion and a sauce made with white wine and mirabelle plums; *de veau Pojarski*, minced veal and bread shaped into a cutlet and fried

côtelette cutlet; (*d'agneau*) *à la turque* (Turkish-style), sautéed lamb, served with tomato and garlic sauce and rice; (*de mouton*) *Champvallon*, mutton, baked between layers of potato and onion; *parisienne* (Paris-style), 'false cutlet' taken from rib of veal and usually slow-cooked (also known as *tendron de veau*); *de saumon Pojarski*, salmon and bread shaped into cutlet and fried; *de volaille*, sliced chicken breast

cotriade white fish stew containing various types of fish and shellfish, potatoes and onions (speciality of Brittany)

cou neck; *d'oie farci*, of (fattened) goose, stuffed with sausage meat, duck liver and truffles, served hot or cold with salad (speciality of Périgord)

Couhé-Vérac goat's-milk cheese, wrapped in leaves, from the Poitou region

coulibiac de saumon (de volaille) pastry filled with salmon or chicken, served hot

coulis purée

Coulommiers creamy white cow's-milk cheese, like a small *Brie* but with a taste closer to *Camembert*

coupe dish or glass for desserts; ice-cream dessert, especially ice-cream and fruit (glacée); *Jacques*, diced, liqueur-soaked fruit, with lemon and strawberry ice-cream, sprinkled with almonds

European Menu Guide

courge marrow, pumpkin

courgette baby marrow, courgette

couronne crown; *de côtelettes rôties*, crown roast of lamb

court-bouillon stock for cooking fish, made with vegetables
and either vinegar or white wine

couscous Arab dish of steamed semolina, meat and
vegetables. served with a sauce poured over

crabe crab; *à l'anglaise* (English-style), dressed

crapiau fruit *crêpe*, speciality of the Nivernais

craquelin biscuit, or oval brioche from the Artois region

Crécy with carrots; carrot soup

crème cream; *à la*, with cream or a cream sauce; *anglaise*,
egg custard; *brûlée*, 'burnt', with a brown sugar topping
heated under the grill until crisp; *caramel*, vanilla custard
with caramel; *Chantilly*, whipped; *glacée*, ice-; *patissière*,
confectioner's custard, custard cream used in various
pastries and dessert dishes

crêpe thin, wheat-flour pancake with either sweet or
savoury filling; *dentelle* ('lace'), very thin, lacy pancakes
made in Brittany; *Suzette*, stuffed with sweet butter filling,
Curaço and orange juice and flamed with cognac

crevette prawn

croissant flaky, crescent-shaped roll made from a dough
containing a high percentage of butter

croquant crunchy petit-four

croque-madame toasted sandwich with ham and fried egg

croque-monsieur toasted sandwich with gruyère cheese
and ham

croquette food (e.g. potatoes) shaped into ovals or
cylinders, covered in egg and breadcrumbs and deep-fried

croustade shell of pastry (otherwise rice, potato or bread)
with filling

croustadine flaky or puff pastry case

croûte ('Crust'), a slice of bread or brioche, fried or baked,
or a pastry covering for a piece of meat; *savoyarde*, puff
pastry topped first with ham then cheese sauce and grilled

croûtons small cubes of fried bread, garnish for soups,
stews or sometimes salad

cru raw

crudité raw vegetables served as an appetizer with a

dipping sauce or mayonnaise

crustacés crustaceans

cuisse ('thigh'), frog's leg, chicken drumstick

cuisseau leg (of veal)

culotte rump (of beef)

cultivateur thick country soup with vegetables, bread and sometimes bacon

dard dace

dariole small pastry usually with a sweet filling such as macaroon and liqueur-flavoured cream

darne fish steak, especially of salmon

datte date; *de mer*, small shellfish

daube stewed or braised meat, game, fish or poultry, but especially beef with red wine and vegetables (*boeuf en*); *provençale*, beef with tomatoes, olives onions and mushrooms

dauphin see *pommes*

dauphine, à la with a garnish of fried croquette potatoes; see also *pommes*

dauphinois see *gratin*

defarde, deffarde stew made with lamb tripe, offal and trotters (speciality of the Dauphiné)

demi-glace ('half-glaze'), rich brown sauce with a meat stock base, sometimes incorporating sherry or madeira

demoiselles de Caen/Cherbourg scampi, cooked and served in *court-bouillon*

diable, à la devilled, hot-flavoured; with sauce containing vinegar, herbs and *demi-glace*, perhaps also with tomatoes and shallots; or with a mustard-based sauce

diablotin ('imp'), peppered cheese toast, to accompany soup

diane pepper sauce with cream, served with venison and steak

dieppoise, à la Dieppe-style, cooked in white wine and garnished with shrimps and mussels (usually applies to salt-water fish)

dijonnaise, à la Dijon-style, with mustard (occasionally, with blackcurrants)

dinde, dindo turkey (hem), turkey (cock); *à la crème*, roasted with a sauce of vegetables and double cream

European Menu Guide

dindonneau young turkey

diplomate (1) sauce for fish, with lobster and mushrooms or truffles: (2) garnish of sweetbreads and mushrooms in madeira sauce: (3) sponge pudding, generally with chocolate and strawberries in layers, covered in cream with vanilla, or with custard and crystallized fruit

Doria garnish of cucumber

douillons pear turnovers made with whole pears (speciality of Normandy)

dragée sugared almond

Dubarry garnish of cauliflower, with or without cheese sauce

duchesse, à la duchess-style: (1) savoury pastry puff: (2) (potatoes), puréed, mixed with egg yolks, shaped and baked

dugléré white wine, cream, onion and tomato sauce for poached fish

duxelles sauce made with onion, white wine and chopped parsley; basis for sauces made with mushroom and shallot cooked in butter

eau water; *douce*, fresh; *gazeuse*, sparkling; *minérale*, mineral; *naturelle*, still; *potable*, drinking; *de Seltz*, soda

eau-de-vie ('water of life'), general name for spirit, especially brandy

écaille shell of oyster)

échalote shallot

échine loin, chine (of pork)

éclade (de moules) mussels roasted over pine needles (specialtiy of Charentes)

éclair long choux pastry with cream or custard filling

écrevisse crayfish (large freshwater prawn); *gratin de queues d'*, tails, cooked in *court-bouillon*, mixed with béchamel and cream and served *au gratin* (speciality of the Dauphiné)

eglefin, egrefin see *aiglefin*

elzekaria Basque soup made with haricot beans, onion, cabbage and garlic

embeurré de chou fresh boiled cabbage, pressed to dry and mixed with butter (speciality of Poitou)

émincé thinly sliced meat covered with a sauce and re-heated

enchaud pork terrine with garlic (speciality of Périgord)

endive chicory

entrecôte ('between the rib'), rib steak; *béarnaise*, with béarnaise sauce; *bordelaise*, with bordelaise sauce; *Mirabeau*, grilled, topped with anchovies and served with anchovy butter and olives

épaule shoulder (e.g. *d'agneau*, *de veau*)

épice spice; *pain d'*, gingerbread

épigramme ('epigram'), either the eye of a lamb cutlet or two different cuts of lamb served together or two pieces of lamb cooked in different ways

épinards spinach

épinée loin, or chine (e.g. *de porc*)

escalope veal cutlet (exceptionally, other meat or fish); *de veau Brillat-Savarin*, veal, flamed in cognac, with a cream and mushroom sauce; *de veau cordon bleu*, veal, stuffed with cheese and ham; *de veau milanaise* (Milan-style), breaded veal, sautéed and served with macaroni, tomatoes and mushrooms; *de veau normande* (Normandy-style), with calvados, cream and apple; *de veau viennoise* (Viennese), breaded veal, sautéed and served with lemon

escargots snails; *à l'alsacienne* (Alsace-style), cooked in a *bouillon* made with Alsatian wine, filled with spiced butter and *fines herbes*; *à l'arlesienne* (Arles-style), cooked in white wine with garlic, served with madeira sauce; *à la bourguignonne* (Bourgogne-style), with herbed garlic butter; *à la chablisienne* (Chablis-style), stuffed with shallots, cooked in white wine, served with herbed garlic butter; *à la vigneronne* (wine-grower's-style), fried in walnut oil, cooked in white wine with shallots and garlic

escarole curly endive

estouffade meat stew with wine, vegetables and herbs

estragon tarragon

esturgeon sturgeon

étuvée same as *estouffade*

fagots meatballs made with liver and fat (speciality of Charentes)

faisan pheasant

farce forcemeat, stuffing

farci stuffed; *poitevin* (Poitou-style), vegetable pâté cooked in *bouillon* and served either hot or cold

farcis niçois aubergines, tomatoes, courgettes and onions, stuffed with bits of meat, eggs, garlic and their own pulp and stewed in oil (speciality of Nice)

farçon (1) in the Auvergne, a large pancake made with fried sausage and vegetables: (2) in the Dauphiné, a large spiced sausage: (3) in the Savoie, potatoes baked *au gratin* with milk and eggs, sometimes also including prunes and bacon

farine flour; *d'avoine*, oatmeal; *de froment*, wheat; *de maïs*, maize; *de sarrasin*, buckwheat; *de seigle*, rye

faux-filet 'false fillet', part of beef sirloin

fechun stuffed cabbage (speciality of the Franch-Comté)

fenouil fennel; *tubereux*, Florence fennel

feuilletée (filled) puff pastry

fève broad bean

ficelle ('string'), long thin loaf; *normande* (Norman), pancake stuffed with creamed ham or mushrooms

figatelli sausages made of pork liver (Corsican speciality)

figue fig

filet fillet; *de boeuf*, of beef; *mignon*, small steak

financière, à la (financier's-style) garnished with cockscombs and kidneys; sauce made with madeira and truffles or truffle essence

fines herbes herb mixture, including parsley, tarragon, marjoram, chives and chervil

fissurelle small shellfish

flageolet flageolet bean

flamande, à la Flemish style, denoting one of several garnishes: braised cabbage, pork or sausage, carrots, turnips and boiled potatoes; red cabbage; red wine, vinegar and onions, etc

flambé flamed, sprinkled with cognac or other spirit, and set alight

flan open tart, sweet or savoury; *aux oignons*, onion tart, speciality of Alsace

flet flounder

flétan halibut

fleurs flowers; *pralinées*, candied flower petals (speciality of Grasse)

fleurons small crescents of puff pastry used to garnish soups and meat dishes

florentine, à la Florence-style, served with spinach

flûte bread roll

foie liver; *gras*, ('fat') goose, from specially fattened birds force-fed with maize; *à l'étuvée*, braised with cognac and vegetables; *de veau à l'anglaise*, calf's, English-style, grilled with slices of bacon

foin, au cooked in hay

fond bottom (e.g. of artichoke)

fondu of cheese, processed

fondu au marc, or au raisin same as *tomme aux raisins*

fondue (1) of vegetables, cooked to a pulp with butter: (2) dish (sometimes described as *au fromage*) of scrambled eggs and gruyère cheese, into which pieces of bread are dipped on skewers by the diners; *bourguignonne* (Burgundian', though in fact of Swiss origin), pieces of tender meat, such as fillet steak, dipped on skewers in a container of boiling oil by the diners, and eaten with various sauces

fontainebleau, (à la) (1) fresh unsalted cream cheese, rich and firm, often served as a dessert with sugar or cream (2) Fontainebleau-style, garnished with small heaps of *duchesse* potato filled with peas, carrots and other vegetables

forestière, à la (forester's-style), garnished with sautéed mushrooms, potatoes and sometimes diced bacon; also rich brown sauce made with mushrooms and flavoured with sherry

fort strong

fouetté whipped (of cream); whisked (of eggs)

fougeru rich cow's-milk cheese, Coulommiers-type, of the Ile-de-France; cured in fern leaves (fern = *fougère*)

four, au In the oven; baked or roasted

fourme ('shape'), name given to group of cheeses from south-western France, suffixed *d'Ambert* (blue-veined, slightly musty-smelling, nicknamed the French Stilton), *de Cantal*, *de Laguiole*, *de Mezenc*, *de Montbrison*, *de Pierre-su-Haute*, *de Rochefort* and *de Salers*

foyot béarnaise sauce with tomato

frais cool, fresh

fraise strawberry; *de bois* (wood), wild

European Menu Guide

framboise raspberry

française, à la French-style, garnished with Anna potatoes and spinach

frangipane pastry cream with chopped almonds and macaroons, used to fill *crêpes*

frappé iced (of desserts, drinks and fruit)

friand small pastry with sweet or savoury filling; *de Saint-Flour*, small sausagemeat pâtés wrapped in leaves

fricandeau (1) veal stew or braise, on a bed of chicory and sorrel: (2) in the Auvergne, pork pâté cooked in the lining of a sheep's stomach

fricassée braised poultry or veal, previously sautéed, in cream sauce

frisée short for *chicorée frisée*, curly endive

frit(e) fried

frites see *pommes*

friture fried food in general, also small fish served fried, with lemon (e.g. *friture de la Loire*)

froid cold

fromage cheese; *blanc*, fresh, rather liquid cream cheese (not dissimilar to yoghurt) usually served with sugar and/or fruit; *à la crème*, cream cheese; *cuit*, cooked, cream cheese with butter and egg yolks, served hot (speciality of Lorraine); *fondu*, processed; *frais*, ('fresh'), medium-fat cheese, similar to fromage blanc and used in similar ways; *de tête de porc*, pig's brawn

fromage '*fromage*' means, literally, 'moulded': otherwise may denote cheesecake, speciality of Charentes

froment wheat or wheat flour

frotée bacon and egg tart from Lorraine, similar to a *quiche*

fruits fruit; *confits*, crystallized; *de mer*, seafood; *rafraîchis*, salad

fumé smoked, cured

fumée de moules same as *éclade*

gâche brioche, in western France

galantine boned poultry, game, meat or fish, stuffed, pressed into shape, cooked in a gelatine broth and served cold

galette (1) flat circular cake or pastry, or open tart, wither savoury or sweet: (2) in Brittany, thick pancake, usually

made of buckwheat flour (*farine de sarrasin*) instead of wheat flour, and often with a savoury filling (see *crêpe*)

galette de la Chaise-Dieu strong goat's-milk cheese of the Auvergne

galicien rich cake flavoured with pistachio nuts

galopiau, galopin thick *crêpe* made with pieces of brioche or bread (speciality of northern France)

gamba large prawn

gaperon d'Auvergne soft cow's-milk (often buttermilk, *gape*) cheese flavoured with garlic

garbure thick country vegetable soup, with a little meat or poultry cooked in it and served separately, as a piece (Gascony region)

garciaux small eels, smoked, tossed in butter and served with cider (speciality of Brittany)

gardon roach

garni garnished, e.g. with vegetables

garniture garnish, usually denoting vegetables

gâteau elaborate cake served as a dessert; *basque*, thick tart filled with *crème patissière*; *battu*, type of brioche; *breton*, large crumbly cake, or tart with apples and cherries; *de Savoie*, light sponge cake

gaudes porridge made with oats, buckwheat or maize flour, according to region, and enriched with cream, served either hot or cold and sliced (speciality of Burgundy and Franche-Comté)

gaufre waffle

gelée jelly

gendarme smoked herring

genièvre, baies de juniper berries

genoese, genoise sponge cake filled with chocolate or fruits

germiny soup made with cream, sorrel and egg yolk

gibier game; *d'eau*, wild water fowl; *de plume*, feathered (birds)

gigorit pig's head stewed in wine and its own blood (Poitou region)

gigot leg (of lamb or mutton)

gigue haunch of venison (or wild boar)

glaçage icing

European Menu Guide

glace ice-cream; *au café*, coffee; *au chocolat*, chocolate

glacé frozen; iced (of cake); glazed

grogues rustic meat pudding with herbs made in the Anjou region

gougère choux pastry encasing a creamy egg-and-gruyère filling

goujon strip (of sole), fried

grand veneur ('great hunter'), sauce with vegetable stock, vinegar, currant jelly and cream

granité Italian water ice, slightly sweetened with sugar

gras-double tripe; *à la lyonnaise* (Lyon-style), with onions and parsley

gratin, gratiné encrusted, usually with breadcrumbs and/or a hard grating cheese

gratin dauphinois sliced potatoes baked with milk and cream and often also grated gruyère

grenade pomegranate

grenouilles frogs; *frites*, deep-fried legs; *à la mode de Boulay*, breaded legs baked with shallots, lemon and parsley; *à la luçonnaise*, Luçon-style, fried frog's legs, previously marinated in vinegar, with garlic (speciality of the Poitou region)

gribiche (1) cold herbed sauce with hard-boiled egg yolks, oil and vinegar: (2) mayonnaise containing chopped hard-boiled eggs, capers, herbs and pickles

grillade grilled dish or toasted sandwich; *au fenouil*, with fennel (fish grilled on leaves)

grillé grilled or toasted

grillons goose or pork scraps that remain after cooking *confits* (speciality of Périgord)

griset black bream (sea fish)

grive thrush, often as a *terrine*

groseille redcurrant; *à maquereau*, gooseberry

grondin gurnard (sea fish)

gruyère generic name for Emmental and similar cheeses

guenilles ('rags'), fritters (speciality of the Auvergne)

haché chopped

hachis minced meat, often served in a sauce; *parmentier*, shepherd's pie

hachua Basque stew made with Bayonne ham, veal or beef,

onions and peppercorns

halicot (or haricot) de mouton (Irish-type) mutton stew

hareng herring; *blanc* (or *salé*), salt; *fumé*, smoked, served cold; *mariné à la fécampoise*, Fécamp style, marinated, preserved with boiling vinegar and wine with lemon slices and vegetables, served cold; *roulé*, rollmop; *à la quimperlaise*, Quimper-style, grilled, and served with a mustard sauce

haricots haricot beans; *blancs à la bretonne* (Brittany-style), with onions browned in butter, tomatoes and garlic; *blanc frais*, fresh; *blanc secs*, dried; *d'Espagne* (Spanish), runner; *verts*, green (French)

hochepot thick soup of Flemish origin with bits of pig meat, salt pork, beef and mutton, cabbage and various root vegetables

hollandaise light béarnaise sauce without shallots or tarragon, but with lemon juice

homard lobster; *à l'armoricaine* (*à l'americaine*), Breton-style (American-style), cooked in oil, with tomatoes and shallots; *à la parisienne*, Paris-style, meat served (cold) in the shell with mayonnaise; *Newburg*, pieces, with cognac, sherry or madeira and cream; *Thermidor*, split in two, cooked au gratin flavoured with mustard and served with a wine sauce

hongroise, à la Hungarian-style, with paprika and usually also tomatoes and onions, often with a soured cream sauce

huile oil

huîtres oysters; *à la bordelaise*, Bordelais-style, with sausage; *Colbert*, fried; *en écaille*, in the shell; *à la Monselet*, threaded on skewers and fried; *villeroi*, coated with white sauce, egg and breadcrumbs and deep-fried

hure (de porc, de sanglier) (pig's, wild boar's) head, usually served as jellied brawn; *blanche*, Alsatian sausage made with pig's head and ham knuckle; *de porc à la parisienne*, pig tongues, Paris-style, in aspic

ile flottante (1) caramelized *oeufs à la neige* served with almonds: (2) sponge cake soaked in kirsch, layered with preserve, covered with whipped cream and floated in vanilla custard

imbrucciate Corsican white cheese tart

impératrice, à l' (Empress-style), rice-based dessert or cake

jambon ham; *à la bayonnaise* (Bayonne-style), cooked in madeira with tomatoes, mushrooms, sausage and rice; *de Bayonne*, smoked Bayonne ham; *braisé à la lie de vin*, boiled, then braised in the lees of red wine with herbs and vegetables (speciality of Burgundy); *cru*, raw (usually salted and smoked); *de Parme* (from Parma in Italy), very thinly sliced raw ham; *persillé*, with parsley, cooked in white wine and served cold in aspic (Burgundy speciality for Easter)

jardinière, à la (in the style of the gardener's wife), with diced mixed vegetables

jésus (de morteau) large smoked pork liver sausage, speciality of Franche-Comté region, with a peg at one end showing that it has been smoked, over juniper and pine wood

Joinville (1) sauce for fish, with egg yolk, cream and purées of crayfish and shrimp, sometimes with diced truffle: (2) boned chicken, stuffed with cream, egg whites, sweetbreads and truffles and casseroled, served with a sauce of the juices, verbena liqueur and brandy

juilienne (1) vegetable consommé: (2) shreds or delicate strips of vegetables or other food

jus juice; *de fruits*, fruit

Kiev, à la Kiev-style; *poulet*, deep-fried boned breasts encasing herb butter

kirsch spirit made with wild cherries, often used in fruit desserts

lait milk

laitance, laite soft roe (of fish)

laitue lettuce; *romaine*, cos

langouste spiny lobster, crayfish, usually served boiled or stewed; *à la calvaise* (Calvi-style), in a highly spiced tomato sauce; *à la parisienne*, Paris-style, served cold with mayonnaise; *Newburg*, sautéed with cognac, madeira and cream; *Thermidor*, cooked in the shell with wine sauce

langoustine large prawns, scampi

langue tongue; *de boeuf*, ox; *de chat* (cat's tongue), long, thin, crisp biscuit

languedocienne, à la Languedoc-style, with garlic, sometimes also with tomatoes, aubergines or *cèpes*

lapereau baby rabbit; *en blanquette*, stewed

lapin rabbit; *à la flamande* (Flanders-style) marinated in red wine, braised with prunes and olives; *aux raisins*, with grapes

lard bacon or pork fat; *de poitrine*, salted or smoked belly of pork

lardon rasher strip (of bacon or pork fat)

laurier bay (leaves)

lentilles lentils

levraut leveret (young hare)

liègoise, à la Liège-style; with juniper berries, or sometimes gin

lièvre hare; *à la broche* (Bourbonnais), marinated and cooked on the spit; *farci en cabessal*, stuffed with highly spiced mixture of veal, pork and ham, shallots and garlic, and cooked in wine (originally from Limousin); *à la périgourdine* or *à la royale* (Périgord-style, royal style), stuffed with *foie gras* and truffles, cooked in wine and cognac (originally from Limousin)

limon lime

limousine, à la Limousin-style, accompanied by braised red cabbage and chestnuts

lit bed (e.g. *lit d'oignons*)

livarot spicy, pungent, cow's-milk cheese from Normandy

livèche lovage

lompe lumpfish

lonzo dried and salted raw ham, made from pork fillet (speciality of Corsica)

lorette with asparagus, chicken croquettes and truffles

lorraine Lorraine-style; *oeufs à la*, eggs baked with bacon, cream and cheese; see also *quiche*

lotte monkfish; *à la marseillaise*, Marseille-style, cooked with cheese, tomato and saffron

lyonnaise Lyon-style, with onions; see *pommes de terre*

macaire see *pommes de terre*

macaron macaroon

macédoine (de fruits, de legumes) ('miscellany'), mixture of fruit or vegetables, raw or cooked, served hot or cold (fresh fruit salad, in its own juice, vegetables with mayonnaise or dressing)

madeleine small fluted sponge-cake, originally from Lorraine

madère madeira

madrilene, à la Madrid-style, tomato-flavoured; *consommé*, clear chicken broth flavoured with tomato juice and usually also peppers and celery

magret, maigret breast fillet of fattened duck, usually lightly grilled or fried

maigre thin, lean, low-fat

maillot, à la mixed vegetable garnish including carrots, turnips, glazed onions, braised lettuce, French beans and peas, usually served with ham

maïs maize, sweetcorn

maison house; *à la, de la*, homemade, house speciality

maître d'hôtel see *beurre*

malouine, à la Saint-Malo-style

maltaise Maltese-style, with oranges; *Hollandaise* sauce made with zest and juice of blood orange

mange-tout ('eat-all'), sugar pea, the pod of which is eaten in addition to the 'peas' inside

maquereau mackerel; *aigre-doux*, sweet and sour, simmered with vinegar, sugar and vegetables; *à la façon de quimper*, served cold with egg and herb sauce; *grillé*, grilled; *maître d'hôtel*, sautéed in butter, sprinkled with lemon juice.

marc spirit distilled from grape residue

marcassin young boar; *à la Saint-Hubert*, roast cutlets with mushrooms

maréchale, à la garnished with asparagus tips and truffles

marée fresh seafood

Marengo cooked in white wine with tomatoes and herbs; see also *poulet*, *veau*

mariné marinated; pickled

marinière, à la mariner's-style, cooked in white wine, with shallots and herbs (especially mussels)

marinoun
very large sausage (speciality of Languedoc)

marjolaine marjoram

marmande type of tomato

marmelade purée of fruit; *en*, cooked to a pulp

marmite large cooking pot used, e.g. for *pot-au-feu*; stew cooked in it; *bressane*, Bresse-style, poached chicked; *dieppoise*, Dieppe-style, fish stew with vegetables, wine and cream

maroilles strong, reddish-rinded, cream-coloured cow's-milk cheese made in northern France

marron chestnut; *glacé*, preserved, glazed and sweet

massepain marzipan

matelote rich mixed fish stew, usually with wine; sauce made with fish stock and wine

mayonnaise dressing made with egg yolk and oil, served cold

médaillon medallion, round cut of meat (see *noisette* and *tournedos*) or other food

Melba see *pêche*

melon melon; *au porto*, chilled and served with port

menouille salt pork, served with potaotes, beans and onions

menthe mint

meringue stiffly beaten egg whites and sugar, baked in a low oven until crisp, served with cream and sometimes fruit

merlan whiting; *en colère* ('angry'), fried, presented with its tail in its mouth; *à la française* (French-style), fillets fried and served with tomato sauce

merlu hake; *à la koskera* (Basque speciality), cooked with asparagus, peas, garlic and potatoes

meunière (Miller's-style), of fish, coated with flour, fried in butter, served with the pan juices

meurette sauce with red wine and butter, served with fresh-water fish and poached eggs

mi-chèvre general name for cheese made of half (minimum 25%) goat's, half cow's milk (or cream), producing a light, rich, aromatic result

miel honey

milanaise, à la Milan-style, with an egg-and-breadcrumb coating, served with parmesan cheese

mille-feuille ('thousand leaves'), puff pastry layered with jam and cream or (less usually) with savoury items

European Menu Guide

Mirabeau, à la with anchovies

mirabelle small yellow plum

mirepoix diced vegetables cooked in butter as a base for sauces and stews

miroton stew made with cooked meat and onions

mode (de), à la in the style (of)

moka mocha, coffee-flavoured

monsieur, fromage de or Monsieur-Fromage (Mr Cheese), fruity cow's-milk cheese made in Normandy, of similar type to Brie though richer and stronger

Mont Blanc sweet dish made with chestnut purée and cream

Montmorency, à la with cherries

mornay béchamel sauce with grated cheese

morue dry salt cod, also known as stockfish; *à la languedocienne*, Languedoc-style, cooked with potatoes and garlic until completely combined

mouclade mussels, with cream, egg yolks and white wine

moules mussels; *à l'armoricaine*, Brittany-style, with onions and tomatoes; *barbues* ('bearded'), larger type of mussel; *à la camarguaise*, Camargue-style, with white wine and lemon mayonnaise; *marinière*, mariner's-style, cooked unshelled with white wine, shallots and parsley; *poulette*, with *sauce poulette*

mousse mousse, frothy sweet or savoury egg mixture; *au chocolat*, chocolate; *au citron*, lemon

mousseline *hollandaise* sauce lightened with whipped cream or egg-whites; *pommes de terre*, potatoes creamed with milk and butter

mousseuse sauce made with butter, lemon juice and egg yolks

mousseux sparkling (of wine)

moutarde mustard

mouton mutton, sheep; *à la bretonne*, Brittany-style, braised and served with haricots

mûre blackberry

mulet grey mullet

Munster, Münster strong, spicy, smelly cheese made in Alsace

muscle Provençal name for mussel

mye type of clam, found particularly on the Atlantic coast

myrtille bilberrry

nage, à la ('swimming'), cooked in an aromatic *court-bouillon*

Nantua Nantua-style, with crayfish; *sauce*, cream sauce with crayfish and butter

Navarin lamb or mutton stew with small onions, potatoes and other vegetables, sometimes called *à la printanière*

navet turnips

nesselrode ice-cream into which are beaten puréed chestnuts and, optionally, candied fruit and liqueur

Neufchâtel soft, white, cow's-milk cheese made in Normandy, medium-to-strong in flavour according to age

Newburg see *homard*

niçoise Nice-style, generally with tomatoes, garlic, olives and capers, sometimes also anchovies, French beans and/or artichokes

nivernaise, à la Nivernais-style, with turnips and carrots

noisettes hazelnuts; also, small, tender pieces of rib or loin

noix nuts, walnuts

normande, à la Normandy-style, with cream, or apples, or calvados, or cider; *sauce*, made with white wine and cream, to accompany fish.

nougat chewy sweet made with roasted almonds and honey

oeufs eggs; *à l'auvergnate*, Auvergne-style, poached, served on cabbage with fried sausage; *brouillés*, scrambled, *à la périgourdine* or *Rossini*, with truffles and *foie gras*; *en cocotte*, baked in ramekins (small ovenproof dishes), sometimes with cream; *à la coque*, soft-boiled; *durs*, hard-boiled; *farcis*, stuffed; *au four*, baked; *frits*, fried; *à la bayonnaise*, with Bayonne ham, *à la languedocienne*, Languedoc-style, with fried aubergine and a garlic-and-tomato sauce; *à la neige* (snow eggs), small mounds of beaten egg white poached in milk and served with vanilla custard (see also *île flottante*); *pochés*, poached; *à la poêle*, fried

oignons onions

oie goose, *à l'alsacienne*, Alsace-style, stuffed with sausage, roasted, served with pickled cabbage (sauerkraut), Strasbourg sausages and pork; *à la flamande*, Flanders-style, stuffed, braised and garnished with vegetables; see also *confit*

olive olive

omelette fluffly pancake made of beaten eggs fried in butter; *aux fines herbes*, with finely chopped parsley, tarragon, chervil and chives; *norvégienne* (Norweigian), sweet souffléed omelette filled with ice-cream

orange orange

origan oregano

Orlof with onion sauce and cheese

os bone

oseille sorrel

oursins sea urchins

pain bread; *bis*, brown; *complet*, wholemeal; *d'épice*, gingerbread; *grillé*, toast, *gros*, large, crusty loaf; *petit*, roll; *de seigle*, rye

palmiers small heart-shaped pastry puffs

palombe wild pigeon

palourdes clams; *farcies*, stuffed with shallots, cream and cheese, speciality of Brittany

pamplemousse grapefruit

panais parsnip

pané (a) coated (with)

pannequet small rolled *crêpe* filled with jam

parfait ice-cream made with eggs and whipped cream, with a flavouring

parisienne Paris-style, with potatoes and leeks or other vegetables

parmentier generally denotes potatoes; *hachis*, with minced meat, like shepherd's pie; *potage*, soup made with potatoes and leeks; see also *pommes de terre*

pâte pastry, cake

pâté (1) meat or fish paste; *de campagne*, of the countryside, coarse-textured, usually made with pork; *de foie gras*, of goose liver from force-fed birds; *maison*, of the house, homemade, smooth-textured meat pâté: (2) pie or pastry, sweet or savoury

patissière pastry-cook; *crème*, confectioner's custard, custard cream used in various dessert dishes

paupiettes thin slices of meat wrapped round a savoury

filing to form cork-sized rolls, as for a beef olive

pauvre homme ('poor man'), sauce with onions, vinegar, mustard and tomato

pavé ('paving stone') (1) thick slice of beef steak; (2) mousse or purée, served cold set in a mould

pavé (d'Auge, de Moyaux) spicy, firm-textured cheese made in Normandy

paysane ('peasant-' or country-style) meat or poultry, usually braised, and garnished with sliced, lightly cooked carrots and turnips, plus onions, bacon and potatoes

pebronata spicy Corsican beef stew

pêche peach; *Melba*, served with ice-cream and raspberry sauce

perdreau partridge

périgourdine, à la Persian-style; *côtelette*, with aubergines, sweet peppers and tomatoes; *sole*, with sweet peppers, rice, lobster sauce and paprika

persil parsley

petite marmite clear meat soup served in individual earthenware dish or *marmite*

petit four ('little oven'), small biscuit or sweet, flavoured with almond, chocolate, etc. and served at the end of the meal

petit pain (bread) roll

petit salé salt pork

petits pois small, young peas

Petit-Suisse fresh, cream-enriched, unsalted cheese made throughout France and marketed in small, cylindrical containers; eaten with sugar or fruit

pièce de boeuf top rump of beef

pieds feet; *-de-cheval* ('horses' hooves'), type of oyster; *de porc*, pigs' troters; *de mouton*, sheep's

piemontaise, à la Piedmont-style, with mushroom (formerly truffle) risotto

pigeon pigeon; *en crapaudine*, flattened slightly and grilled

pilaf, pilau, pilaw pilau (flavoured) rice

pilon drumstick (poultry)

piment pimento, sweet red or green pepper, capsicum

pintade guinea-fowl

pipérade lightly scrambled eggs with fried tomatoes,

peppers, onions and basil, oftern served with Bayonne ham (Basque speciality)

piquante sauce with shallots, white wine, vinegar, pickles and herbs

pirojki small croquettes filled with cheese or minced game, fish or vegetables (of Russian origin)

pissaladière tart with onions, black olives, anchovies and often tomatoes (speciality of Nice)

pistache pistachio nut

plateau platter, tray, large plate (e.g. for seafood or cheeses)

plombières ice-cream with vanilla kirsch, candied fruit and *crème Chantilly*; or almond ice-cream with apricot jam

pluvier plover

pochouse stew made with freshwater fish, especially eel, cooked with white wine (speciality of Bourgogne)

point, à (of steak), medium rare; (of fruit or cheese), just ripe or ready to eat

pointe tip (e.g. of asparagus)

poire pears; *belle dijonnaise*, poached and served with blackcurrant ice-cream and sauce; *belle-Hélène*, poached, served with vanilla ice-cream and topped with a hot chocolate sauce; *vigneronne*, or *au vin rouge*, in red wine

poireaux leeks; à la niçose (Nice-style), cooked in oil, with tomatoes and garlic

pois pea(s); *cassés*, split; *chiche*, chick-pea; *princesse*, mange-touts

poisson fish

poitrine breast; *d'agneau*, lamb; *de boeuf*, brisket of beef; *de porc*, belly of pork

poivrade game sauce made with meat juices, pepper and vinegar

poivre pepper; *blanc*, white; *de Cayenne*, cayenne; *gris* or *noir*, black; *vert*, green peppercorns

poivre d'Auvergne black-coated cheese of the *tomme* family, moderately flavoured with black pepper

poivron capsicum, sweet red or green pepper

pojarski cutlet assembled from chopped meat or fish and fried

polonaise Polish-style, with a garnish of sieved hard-boiled egg yolks and breadcrumbs in butter

pommes apples

pommes (de terre) potatoes; *allumettes*, matchsticks, fried; *à l'anglaise*, English-style, peeled and boiled; *Anna*, pancake of layered slices of potato, fried; *à la basquaise*, Basque-style, hollowed out and filled with tomato, pimentos and ham, baked with a breadcrumb topping; *boulangère* (baker's-style), cooked with onions in butter and baked with onions; *château*, whole, small oval potatoes sautéed in butter; *dauphin*, grated and cooked as pancakes; *dauphine*, small crequettes of creamed potato, breaded and fried; *duchesse*, puréed with egg yolks, glazed and browned in the oven; *frites*, fried (chips); *frites chip*, game chips; *impériale*, baked in their skins with butter, cream and mushrooms; *lyonnaise*, sliced and sautéed with onions; *macaire*, mashed with butter, shaped and baked; *mousseline*, mashed, with whipped cream; *noisette*, as *pommes château* with smaller potatoes the size of large hazelnuts; *à la normande*, cooked with onions and leeks in butter and browned; *paille*, sliced like straw (*paille*) and fried; *à la parisienne*, small, rolled in meat jelly; *parmentier*, diced and cooked in butter; *Pont-Neuf*, fried (chips); *en robe de chambre* (in a dressing-gown) or *en robe des champs* (in field garb), boiled, steamed or baked unpeeled; *sarladaise* (from Sarlat in Périgord), sliced, cooked in the oven with goose fat and sometimes truffles; *savoyarde*, as *boulangère*, with the addition of bacon and a topping of grated cheese

porc pork; *carré de porc à la périgourdine*, cold boned loin, braised in wine with truffles; *côtes de porc à l'ardennaise* (Ardennes-style), pork chops with juniper berries; *noisettes de*, *aux pruneaux*, thick pieces of pork cooked with prunes served with a rich redcurrant sauce (Touraine speciality)

Pont-l'Evèque sweet-flavoured, tangy, strong-smelling cow's-milk cheese from Normandy

porcelet suckling pig

Port (de) Salut milk cow's-milk cheese made throughout France (variety of Saint-Paulin)

portugaise (Portuguese), with tomatoes cooked with garlic and onions

(petit) pot-au-crème, de chocolat light dessert, served in

European Menu Guide

small individual dishes, of cream mixed with egg yolks and various flavourings

potage thick country soup

pot-au-feu ('pot on the fire'), classic two-course dish, beef broth followed by boiled beef and fresh vegetables, e.g. onions, carrots, leeks and trunips (many regional variants, including substitution of poultry for meat); *à la carcassone*, Carcassonne-style, with, in addition, bacon, stuffed cabbage and haricots; *à la languedocienne*, Languedoc-style, with, in addition, salt pork

potée mixed vegetable and meat soup; *auvergnate* (Auvergne-style), with beans, pig's head, *cervelas*, pork belly or salt pork, cabbage, potatoes and various other vegetables, poured over dried bread; *bretonne* (Brittany-style), with pork, sausage, cabbage and carrot

pouding (substantial) pudding (not any dessert dish)

poularde pullet; *au blanc*, poached, with cream sauce; *demi-deuil* (half-mourning), studded with truffles and poached; *Tosca*, pot-roasted with fennel

poule hen; *au pot*, stuffed and poached, with vegetables

poule de mer John Dory

poulet chicken; *à l'alsacienne*, Alsace-style, with noodles, peas and parmesan cheese; *basquaise*, Basque-style, casseroled with tomatoes, peppers, mushrooms and peppercorns; *à la bohemienne* (Bohemian-style), with mushrooms, artichokes and herbs; *Carmen*, boned roast, with a mayonnaise sauce incorporating red peppers, peas, mustard and rice; *à l'estragon*, poached, with tarragon; *en gelée*, in aspic; *(à la) Kiev*, boned breasts deep-fried with herb or garlic butter inside; *Marengo*, sautéed with tomatoes, garlic and mushrooms (and, theoretically, fried egg, crayfish tails and croûtons); *(sauté) à la provençale*, Provence-style, fried with tomatoes, onions, garlic, white wine, served with olives, mushrooms and anchovies; *vallée d'Auge*, with cream and tiny onions

poulette (1) pullet, young chicken; (2) *velouté* sauce with lemon juice, parsley and sometimes mushrooms

pousse-café short-drink (spirit) taken after coffee

poussin very young, small chicken, usually served as an individual portion

poutassou blue whiting

praline praline, mixture of toasted ground nuts, usually almonds, and sugar, added to dessert dishes

pressé pressed; *citron*, freshly squeezed lemon juice

pression ('pressure'), draught (beer)

primeurs first, or early, vegetables

princesse, à la ('Princess-style'), garnished with asparagus tips, artichoke and small potatoes

printanier (printanière, à la) ('Spring-style'), diced carrots or turnips, blanched, with peas and French beans; see also *Navarin*

profiteroles profiteroles, small balls or fingers of choux pastry filled with custard or whipped cream, covered with chocolate (*au chocolat*) or other sauce

provençale, à la with tomato, and usually garlic and onions

prune plum; *de Damas*, damson

pruneau prune

puits d'amour ('well of love'), small pastry with sweet filling of fruit or cream

purée purée; *argenteuil*, asparagus; *Crécy*, carrots; *parmentier*, potatoes; *de pommes de terre*, mashed potatoes; *Rachel*, artichoke hearts; *Saint-Germain*, peas or split peas; *soubise*, onions; *Vichy*, carrots

quenelles small poached sausage-shaped mousses; *de brochet*, pike; *de volaille*, chicken

queue tail; *de boeuf*; ox; *d'écrevisse*, crayfish

quiche open tart with savoury filling; *lorraine*, Lorraine-style, with eggs, cream and bacon

râble saddle (of hare or rabbit); *de lapin à la moutarde*, speciality of Dijon, rabbit roasted with mustard and served with cream in the sauce

ragoût stew

raie skate; *au beurre noir*, with black butter

raifort horseradish

raisin grape; *de Corinthe*, currant; *de sec*, raisin; *de Smyrne*, sultana

ramier wood-pigeon

râpé grated (cheese)

ratatouille vegetables, such as aubergines, courgettes, tomatoes, peppers, onions, and garlic, cooked in oil and served either hot or cold

ravigote (from the verb *ravigoter*, to enliven), type of vinaigrette with mustard, capers, gherkins, onion, lemon juice and herbs, served cold

Reblochon smooth, sweet, creamy cow's-milk cheese from the Savoie

reine-claude greengage

rémoulade mayonnaise with capers, onions, gherkins and herbs

rhubarbe rhubarb

rhum rum

rillette minced pork cooked in fat (speciality of Touraine)

rillon pieces of pork or goose cooked in fat

ris sweetbreads (calf's or lamb's); *Régence*, calf's braised, with a sauce containing cream, *foie gras*, mushrooms and port

rissole small deep-fried pastry puff with savoury filling

riz rice; *à l'impératrice*, with custard, crystallized fruit and cream, in a mould; *à l'indienne*, Indian-style, boiled; *pilaf*, pilaw, browned in butter with chopped onions

Robert sauce, often served with chops, made with onions, white wine, vinegar and mustard

rognons kidneys; *Beaugé*, in Bordeaux, with madeira and mustard; *vert pré* (green meadow), grilled with butter and parsley, garnished with watercress

rognons de coq kidney beans

Roquefort sharp, salty sheep's-milk cheese, blue, with a buttery texture; made on the Causse plateau

Rossini see *tournedos*

rôti roast; the meat course; *de porc Montmorency*, pork, with a wine and cherry sauce

rouge red

rouget mullet; *à la niçoise*, Nice-style, with tomatoes, anchovies and black olives

roulade roll of meat, fish or other food, sometimes stuffed

roulé rolled

royale coated in cream sauce, with truffles; *consommé*, clear soup with shaped pieces of savoury custard as garnish

rutabaga swede

sabayon ('zabaglione'), sauce of eggs yolks and sugar with wine or liqueur, served warm

safran saffron

saignant underdone, rare (of steak)

Saint-Germain purée of peas or split peas (sometimes also with artichokes)

Saint-Hubert game consommé with white wine

Saint-Marcelli mild-flavoured cow's-milk cheese (formerly made from goat's milk) of the Dauphiné

Sainte-maure strong-flavoured, soft goat's-milk cheese produced in the Touraine in long cylinders

Saint-Michel coffee sponge cake

Saint-Nectaire frim-textured, fruity flavoured cow's-milk cheese from the Auvergne, sometimes stirred into soup

Saint-Paulin mild cow's-milk cheese, made throughout France

salade salad; *folle* ('foolish': *nouvelle* cuisine term), green beans, *foie gras* and shellfish; *Francillon*, mussels, potatoes marinated in Chablis, trufles, hot vinaigrette; *Lorette*, lamb's lettuce, beetroot and celery; *mimosa*, lettuce with orange and hard-boiled egg; *monégasque* (Monaco-style), with tiny fish, tomatoes and rice; *niçoise* (Nice-style), with tomatoes, olives, capers, tuna, hard-boiled eggs and green peppers (many variants exist); *panachée*, mixed; *russe*, (Russian), various vegetables, diced, with mayonnaise; *tiede*, warm; verte, green; *Waldorf*, celery, apple and walnut

salé salt, salted

salpicon pieces of meat or fish with diced vegetables in sauce, used as a stuffing or garnish

sandre fresh-water fish of the Loire

santé ('health'), with potatoes and sorrel

sarrasin buckwheat

sauce sauce

saucisse sausage (type that must be cooked)

saucisson sausage, dried or cooked type

sauge sage

saumon salmon; *blanc*, hake

sauté ('jumped'), *sautéed* or tossed in butter, fried

savarin ring-shaped sponge cake, soaked in syrup and liqueur or spirit

savoyarde, à la (Savoie-style), usually with potatoes, eggs, cream and gruyère cheese

scarole betavian endive

seigle rye

sel salt

selle saddle; *d'agneau*, of lamb; *de chevreuil*, of venison; *de veau*, of veal

semoule semolina; *gâteau de*, pudding, oven-baked and with a jam sauce poured over it

sirop syrup, juice

soissonaise Soissons-style, with haricots

sole sole; *bonne-femme* ('good wife'), poached in white wine with mushrooms and served with potato; *cardinal*, poached, with a cream and crayfish sauce; *dugléré*, poached with a white wine, cream, tomato, parsley and onion sauce; *marguéry*, with white wine, mussels and prawns; *meunière*, coated with flour, fried in butter, served with the pan juices, parsley and lemon; *véronique*, poached in white wine, with grapes to garnish

sorbet water ice, usually fruit-flavoured

soubise béchamel sauce with onion

soufflé ('puffed'), soufflé, light, frothy dish, sweet or savoury, made with eggs and oven-baked; *à l'orange*, orange

soupe soup; *à la bière*, with beer (speciality of Alsace)

spätzel noodles made with eggs (in Alsace)

spetzli rich dumplings, speciality of Alsace, served with butter

spoom water ice, flavoured with wine or fruit juice and mixed with meringue

Stanley with a smooth curry sauce

steack, steak steak; *au poivre*, pepper steak, covered in crushed peppercorns, fried and flambéed in cognac

sucre sugar

sultane, à la garnished with red cabbage and *duchesse* potatoes

suprême (1) breast of chicken; *à la crème*, sautéed, served with a cognac and cream sauce: (2) reduced velouté sauce with cream

tapenade anchovy paste or purée with capers, black olives and tuna

tartare (1) mayonnaise with onions, capers, mustard and chopped chives: (2) steak, raw, minced, and mixed with

tarte tart, with sweet or savoury filling: *alsacienne aux abricots*, apricot pie; *au citron*, lemon tart; *aux fraises*, strawberry tart; *Tatin*, with apples, upside down, caramelised, served hot

tartelette small individual tart

tendrons strips of breast of veal, also known as *côtelettes parisiennes*

terrine coarse-textured pâté; also the dish in which it is cooked

tête head; *de veau*, calf's, often set in aspic, alternatively *en tortue* (see below)

thon tuna or tunny fish

thym thyme

timbale (de) cooked in a mould called a *timbale*

tomates tomatoes; *à la provençale*, halved and baked with a sprinkling of parsley and garlic

tomme family of cheeses produced mainly in Alpine areas, usually from goat's or sheep's milk, and generally smooth in texture and mild in flavour; *aux raisins*, steeped in *marc* (also known as *fondu aux raisins*)

topinambour Jerusalem artichoke

tortoni ice-cream dessert flavoured with rum and almonds

tortue turtle; *en*, in a sauce containing herbs, tomato and madeira; or a soup made with beef stock and pieces of turtle

tournedos thick slices of beef fillet; *cordon rouge*, sautéed with ham and *foie gras*, with a rich port and brandy sauce; *à la monégasque*, Monaco-style, sautéed, with aubergines, black olives and tomato sauce; *Rossini*, with a sauce of truffles, *foie gras* and madeira

tourte (1) pie, tart; *de truffles à la périgourdine*, hot pie filled with truffles and *foie gras* soaked in cognac; (2) round loaf of bread

tripes tripe; *à la mode de Caen*, cooked in cider and calvados, with trotters, vegetables and herbs; *à la niçoise*, Nice-style, beef tripe with vegetables and garlic; pork and beef tripe in tomato sauce

truffes truffles; *sous la cendre*, wrapped in oiled paper or tin-foil and cooked under ashes, or wrapped in dough and

European Menu Guide

baked; or wrapped in a thin slice of fresh bacon and oiled paper and cooked under ashes

truite trout; *au bleu*, boiled live in water with vinegar, which makes it turn blue; *meunière*, dipped in flour and sautéed in butter, with parsley and lemon

vacherin ice-cream in a meringue shell

Vallée d'Auge sauce with calvados and cream

veau veal; *ballotine de*, boned, stuffed and braised shoulder; *brochettes de*, grilled skewered veal cubes; *Marengo*, sautéed, in oil with tomatoes, onions and mushrooms; *poitrine de, aux groseilles, verts*, breast, braised with a sauce of white wine and gooseberries

velouté ('velvety'), classic sauce made with white stock and wine; *Yvonne*, cream of chicken soup which includes lettuce

venaison venison; see also *chevreuil*

véronique, à la with white grapes

verte green; *sauce*, mayonnaise with herbs (parsley, tarragon and chervil)

Vichy, à la carrots cooked in Vichy water

viennoise, à la Vienna-style, with capers, parsley, chopped hard-boiled eggs, olives, lemon and butter

villeroi, à la coated with thick mushroom-flavoured sauce *allemande*, egg and breadcrumbs, and fried

vinaigre vinegar

vinaigrette dressing for cold food, made with oil, wine vinegar and seasoning

volaille poultry

vol-au-vent large puff-pastry case, also small individual-sized ones, filled with chopped poultry, fish or shell fish or vegetables in a *velouté* or *béchamel* sauce

Walewska, à la crayfish and truffle garnish, with sauce *mornay*, for fillets of sole

Xavier beef consommé flavoured with madeira, garnished with strips of pancake

xeres sherry

yaourt yoghurt

zingara ('gypsy'), garnish, for veal and fowl, of white wine, mushrooms, tomato sauce and ham

Zola beef consommé, served with tiny cheese and truffle dumplings

Germany

German cuisine is like their welcome, hearty. Their restaurant service is excellent and they are very good at catering for children.

There are three distinct eating places, the formal restaurant, the informal (beer cellars, café) and the Kondotorie which is similar to the English tea shop but instead serves coffee, hot chocolate, tortes and cream cakes. And everything with cream (mit sahne). Many of the traditional dishes in Germany and Austria may strike the traveller as being 'homely' in terms of restaurant fare. In fact, these countries tend to offer far more variations of homely cooking than is found in their British counterparts.

As the Germans prefer hearty, plate-filling dishes, such as thick soups and substantial courses with plenty of different sausages and meat, all eating places serve large helpings. Eating out is a popular pastime with the Germans, they not only take a considerable time to eat, but you will often see whole families dining out rather than just the 'professional businessman'. Like the French, the ingredients of their main dishes might seem at times extravagant but nothing is wasted. Liver from the goose is used in delicious soups and starters as are asparagus stalks, even fruit is not forgotten and the soups made from fruit are delightful.

It would be wrong to think that German food is plain and uninteresting because it is substantial; the reverse is true as it has richness and body coupled with immense variety. There are several regions and the food in each is quite different in flavour as well as presentation. As a whole, the cooking in Germany stems from its pre-unification days. Unlike French cuisine, a regional name of a dish, for example Berliner Kranzkuchen, does not lend itself to any particular ingredient or method of cooking, it merely denotes that the dish originated from a particular region and forms part of its traditional fare. In German cooking, herbs are not added

directly to the cooked food but are infused indirectly via seasoned sausages and meats. Roasts are popular; fish is considered a luxury and what is done with the humble herring is quite unforgettable. But the undoubted favourite must be the different pork meat dishes.

The Germans used to eat five times a day but this has altered giving way to a now slimmer German. There is the first breakfast of rolls with honey and jam, eggs and coffee. Then there is the second breakfast at 11.00am. This is a more elaborate and substantial affair with sausages, other meats, bread, salad, and delicacies, such as smoked salmon and smoked goose breast. Traditional lunchtime fare is also substantial with soups followed by roast and crisp or creamed vegetables, dumplings and/or potatoes; hearty casseroles may also be served. 5.00pm is their tea-time with delicious homemade *tortens*, and tarts, sandwiches (sometimes eaten with a knife and fork). Dinner or supper is a lighter meal and is eaten later.

Austrian cooking is again, different. This can be attributed to the intermingling of peoples and cultures for over 600 years. It is said that *Apfelstrudel* was made by a Turk while laying siege to Vienna in the seventeenth century. Indeed, Austrian cooking shows the world the flavours of Europe. There is a delicacy of taste and it is more highly seasoned than German cuisine – it tantalises the palate and is beautifully presented.

Austrians utilise a lot of eggs in their cooking, pancakes and pudding, *hors d'oeuvres* and appetisers. It is considered the home of coffee and pastries and this practice has now become a social pastime with the Austrians perfecting the 'art'. Both the Germans and Austrians enjoy their dumplings in very many forms from savoury to sweet; boiled, baked, fried and poached – exceptional variety. Indeed the German like for this taste of sweet and sour can be seen in other dishes, sweet and sour red cabbage with apples, onions and diced bacon (Bavaria), *Sauerkraut* with caraway seeds and pork or sausages added.

This section can also be useful for those English residents in Germany or those on self-catering holidays when making up their shopping lists. It is appropriate here to include a word on the German language. Whilst English would have several separate words the Germans often use one compound word and therefore on occasions, it may be necessary to look up separately, two parts of a word.

No excursion into German and Austrian cuisine is complete without sampling their sausages and cheeses complemented by their beers and wines. The different types of *Wurste* (sausages) and *Kase* (cheese) are listed separately and not under their generic headings. Basic drinks (*punches*) are included but wines are not. Where a dish is traditionally eaten at a particular time of year, for example Christmas, then this has been stated.

The German people are hearty and athletic and their menus reflect this characteristic. A gastronomic visit to the land of Wagner's Brühilde and Siegfried is certainly not for the diet-conscious traveller.

Phrases For The Restaurant

I want to reserve a table for..... at.....
Ich möchte einen Tisch für..... Personen für..... Uhr bestellen

Have you a table for.....
Haben Sie einen Tisch für ..... Personen

A quiet table
Einen ruhigen Tisch

A table near the window
Einen Tisch am Fenster

A table on the terrace
Einen Tisch auf der Terrasse

Could we have another table please?
Könnten wir einen anderen Tisch bekommen?

I am in a hurry/we are in a hurry
Ich bin in Eile/Wir sind in Eile

Please bring me the menu
Könnten Sie mir bitte die Speisekarte bringen

Can we have ..... please
Könnten wir bitte ein ..... bekommen

Local dishes
Typische Gerichte aus dieser Gegend

How much is it?
Wievel kostet das?

What is it?
Was ist das?

I did not order this
Ich habe das nicht bestellt

Too much
Zu viel

More
Etwas mehr

The bill please
Die Rechnung, bitte

Is service included?
Ist Bedienung inklusiv?

I think there is a mistake in the bill
Ich glaube, die Rechnung stimmt nicht

Do you accept travellers' cheques?
Kann ich mit Travvellers-Schecks bezahlen?

Restaurant Terms

Abendbrot, Abendessen dinner, supper

aperitif aperitif, drink taken before the meal (to stimulate the appetite)

bar bar, nightclub

Bedienung inbegriffen service included

bestellung order

Bierhalle beer hall; as well as beer, hot meals, sausages, salads and Pretzels are available

Café café, coffee shop, in which one can also buy pastries, snacks and other drinks

einschiesslich included, inclusive

essen dinner, main meal

Fräulein! waitress!

Früstuck breakfast

Gasthaus, Gasthof (in Austria) inn, usually rural, offering home-cooking and a folksy atmosphere

Gaststätte restaurant

Gedeck set menu

glas glass

hauptgericht entrée

hausgemacht home-made

Imbissbar lunch counter or lunch room in a restaurant

inbegriffen included

Inklusive Bedienung service included

Kaffeehaus coffee-house, originally a Vienese institution but now common throughout Austria and Germany; not merely a place to drink coffee but also a social meeting-place, offering pastries of all kinds and often snacks as well

karaffe carafe

Karte menu (the actual card on which the list of available dishes is printed or written)

Kellner waiter

Kellnerin waitress

Konditorei cake shop, which often has a café area for coffee and pastries

Mehrwertsteuer V.A.T. (usually included)

Menü set menu; *Menü essen*, to have one of the set meals,

European Menu Guide

the set menu; *Menü des Tages*, set meal of the day

Milchbar milk bar, selling plain and flavoured milk and pastries

mittagessen lunch

nachtisch dessert

nachtklub night-club

Ober waiter; (*Herr*) Ober! waiter!

portion portion, helping; *eine halbe portion*, a half portion; *eine zweite portion*, a second helping; *eine portion kaffee*, a pot of coffee

raststätte (Rasthof in Austria) motorway restaurant, with overnight service station facilities

Rechnng bill

Restaurant restaurant; mainly in towns, with menus catering for foreign visitors as well as offering local specialities

Schnellimbiss snack bar, selling mainly beer and sausages

Speisekarte menu (the actual card on which the list of available dishes is printed or written)

Speisenfolge order of the menu, the courses

Spezialität des Hauses speciality of the house

Spezialitäten local dishes

Tagesgericht speciality of the day

Tagesmenü set menu

Tisch (1) table; (2) meal

vorspeise appetizer

Weinstube wine bar, especially in wine-producing districts where new wines can be sampled with hot dishes and snacks. Also called Heuriger in Austria

Würstchenstand snack bar selling mainly beer and sausages

zweites frühstuck mid-morning snack, elevenses

zwischengericht entrée

Menu Terms

Aal eel; *Aal in Gelee*, jellied eel; *Aalpalatte Victoria*, smoked eel platter; *Aalsuppe*, soup made from eels, peas, shallots, herbs and white wine, served with pears steamed in red wine and often semolina dumplings; *Hamburger Aalsuppe*, variation of traditional *Aalsuppe*, in which white wine is replaced by beef broth, and the vegetables and herbs used are carrots, leeks and parsley; *Garnierter Aal*, eel and apple salad; *Grüner Aal mit Gurkensalat*, cooked in herbs, served in a creamy sauce with cucumber salad

Allgäuer Bergkäse cow's milk cheese similar to *Emmenthal*; *Allgäuer Limburger*, a mild *Limburger*; *Allgäuer Rahmkäse*, a full cream cow's milk cheese

Alpkäse ('Alpine cheese') smaller variety of *Bergkäse* (see below)

Alsen shad

Ananas pineapple

Anis aniseed

Aperitif aperitif

Apfel apple; *mit Leberfulle*, stuffed with pork, apple, goose liver and herbs, baked in wine; *Apfelauflauf*, apple and almond batter pudding; *Apfelauflauf mit Reis*, apples cooked in wine, topped with creamed rice and meringue; *Apfelbrotsuppe*, apple soup with pumpernickel and currants; *Apfelcreme*, apple cream; *Apfelklösse*, apple and almond dumplings; *Apfelkren*, apple and horseradish sauce; *Apfelkuchen*, rich yeast pastry topped with apple slices; *Apfelkuchen mit Guss*, apple custard cake; *Apfelmuss*, apple purée; *Apfelreis*, boiled rice with apples and sultanas; *Apfelsalat*, apples, raisins and nuts in cream; *Apfelschmarren*, apple pancake, cut into small pieces; *Apfelstrudel*, very thin layers of pastry filled with slice of apple, raisins, nuts and cinnamon; *Badische Apfelrolle*, apples, almonds and raisins in marmalade-covered puff pastry; *Schwäbisher Apfelkuchen*, sweet pastry tart with apple, almond and raisin filling, with an almond topping

Apfelsaft apple juice

Apfelsine orange

European Menu Guide

Apfelwein cider

Appetithäppchen canapes

Aprikose apricot

arme Leute ('poor people') consommé with potatoes and onions

Arme Ritter ('poor knignts') bread soaked in milk, fried in egg and breadcrumbs and flavoured with cinnamon

Art, auf in the style of

Artischocke artichoke; *Artischockenblätter*, filled artichoke leaves; *Artischockenboden*, artichoke bottoms stuffed with either an onion and mushroom sauce, or onion purée

Asche grayling (a popular freshwater fish in Germany)

Aspik aspic

Aubergine aubergine

Auerhahn capercaillie; *Gebratene Auehahn*, capercaillie roasted with juniper berries and white wine and sour cream suace, served with an apple compote

Auflauf pudding (sweet or savoury)

Aufschnitt (assorted) sliced cold meats; *Feiner kalter Aufschnitt*, cold meat platter

Augsburger Würste coars lightly smoked pork sausages seasoned with cloves and nutmeg

Austern oysters; *Austernsuppe*, a thickened wine soup with oysters and anchovies

Avocado (birne), Avocato (birne) avocado (pear)

Backerbsen tiny golden batter balls used as a garnigh for soup

Bäckerei (Austrian) (1) pastries: (2) biscuits; *Weihnachtsbäckerei*, 'Christmas biscuits' are traditional fare in Austria

Backsteinkäse Bavarian cheese similar to *Limburgerkäse* made from full cream cow's milk

Badish Baden-style

Banane banana; *Bananenwasser*, bananas sieved and mixed with rum

Bär bear; fillets are cooked in red wine

Barsch freshwater perch

Basilikum basil

Bauern-, Bauernart, nach peasant-style, usually denoting a fairly simple but substantial dish

Bauern-Caviar cottage cheese mixed with grated Edam, onion and paprika pepper

Bauernfrühstück an enormous meal consisting of scrambled eggs, reheated cooked meats, bacon, mixed vegetables, fried potatoes and fried tomatoes; or in some parts of Germany, mixed garlic sausages

Bauernklösse baked dumplings made with oatmeal, potato, bacon and onion

Bauernomelett diced bacon and onion omelette

Bauernsalat simple salad consisting mainly of shredded white and red cabbage mixed with lettuce and watercress with a sour cream mayonnaise dressing

Bauernschmaus (Austrian) a hearty dish made from pork chops, bacon and sausages, cooked in beer with sauerkraut, potatoes, onions and herbs, and served with breadcrumb dumplings

Bauernsuppe cabbage and frankfurter soup

Bayerisch Bavarian-style; *Bayerischer Jägertopf* ('hunter's casserole'), beef stewed with vegetables in wine

Beefsteak (deutsches) hamburger steak

Beere berry

Belegte Brote open sandwiches, usually of rye bread and sausages

Bergkäse ('mountain cheese') Austrian hard cheese, quite mild when young, but sharper as it matures

Berliner Berlin-style; *ein Berliner*, jam doughnut; *Berliner Kranzkuchen* ('garland cake'), plaited fruit and almond yeast ring cake

Bettelmannsuppe ('beggar's soup') hearty soup of beef and mixed vegetables

Beuschel (Austrian) lights, lungs; usually stewed with root vegetables, lemon, onion and herbs and spices, to which are added capers and anchovies, and finally sour cream. The stew is garnished with dumplings

Biberschwanz beaver's tail (regarded as a delicacy in Germany); fried in an egg and breadcrumb coating, served with slices of lemon

Bienenstich honey-almond cake

Biier beer; *ein dunkles*, a darker beer; *ein helles*, a light beer; *vom fass*, draught bee; *Bierkaltsuppe, Bierkaltschale*, cold soup of light beers with currants, brown breadcrumbs, cinnamon and lemon juice; *Bierkäse* see *Stangenkäse*; *Bierplinse*, batter made with dark beer instead of milk, used for sweet and savoury fritters; *Biersuppe*, beer soup, flavoured with lemon and cinnamon; *Bierwurst*, beer sausage; *Münchner Biercreme*, cold soufflé dessert of beer, lemon juice and eggs

Birne pear

Bishofsbrot ('bishop's bread') fatless cake with dried figs, dates, nuts, candied peel and lemon, sometimes also with chocolate and glacé cherries

Biskuit sponge (fatless); *Biskuitgeback*, sponge cake

Biskuitschöberi-suppe (Austrian) rich beef broth garnished with small light scones

Bismarckhering soused herring with onions

Bismarck-Suppe strong, slightly thickened consommé, flavoured with port, and garnished with diced mushrooms and grated cheese

Blätterteig puff pastry

blau blue; *Blaufisch*, fish poached with vinegar to give a blue sheen; *Blaukraut*, shredded red cabbage braised with wine vinegar, apples, onions and caraway seeds

Blaubeere bilberry, blueberry

Blumenkohl cauliflower; *Gebackener Blumenkohl*, lightly cooked, then baked in a cheese and cream sauce

blutig rare (of steak)

Blutwurst ('blood sausage') black pudding

Bockwurst large frankfurter, boiled

Böhmisch Bohemian-style; *Böhmische Dalken*, rich, sweet dough, served hot, with plum jam or redcurrant jelly in the hollow at the centre of the round

Bohne bean; *grosse Bohnen*, broad beans; *grüne Bohnen*, green, French beans; *Wachsbohnen*, yellow, wax beans; *weisse Bohnen*, white, haricot beans; *Bohnen mit Backpfaumen*, prunes cooked with dried beans; *Bohnensuppe*, bean soup with bacon; *Frankfurter Bohnensuppe*, kidney bean soup with vegetables and sliced frankfurter sausages; *Serbische Bohnensuppe*, sliced bean soup ***with vegetables and smoked sausage

bouillon clear soup

Brachse bream

Brandkrapferlsuppe (Austrian) beef broth with fried
profiteroles

brat- roast; -*braten*, joint, roast

Bratklops rissole, usually served with sauerkraut

Bratwurst fried or braised sausage, usually preceded on
menus by the name of its locality; *Geräucherte Bratwürste*,
smoked sausages made from pork and bacon

Braunkohl broccoli, kale; *Braunkohl Holsteiner Art*, kale with
leeks braised in oatmeal-thickened beef stock

Braunschweiger Brunswick-style; *Braunschweiger Schloss
salat* ('Brunswick Castle salad'), celeriac and truffle salad

Breitling whitebait

Bremer Bremen-style; *Bremen Matrosenfleisch* ('sailor's-
stew'), thick stew of beef and pork with vegetables and
horseradish in red wine

Brennender Pudding ('burning pudding') ring-shaped light
steamed pudding, served with brandy-soaked sugar lumps
in the middle, which are then set alight at the table

Bries sweetbread

Broeselknödel unsweetened small dumplings

brombeere blackberry

Brot bread; many varieties, most of them dark and made
with rye flour; *Roggenbrot*, rye bread; *Schwarzbrot*, black
bread; *Kaffeekuchen*, coffee bread; *Klezenbrot*, meringue
bread, with almonds and sultanas; *Kuchenbrot*, cake bread,
with dried fruit; *Brötchen*, bread roll; *Brotoch*, a delicate,
moulded, steamed pudding covered with almonds and
candied peel and served with a vanilla, lemon or liqueur
sauce; *Brotpudding*, similare to the English bread pudding,
but with ground almonds and grated lemon peel instead of
dried fruits; *Brotsuppe*, thickened soup made with
breadcrumbs and veal stock, served with smoked sausage
cubes; *Ostpreussische Brotsuppe*, sweet-sour of bread,
spices and sugar with sour cream and lemon juice

Brunnenkresse watercress

Buchtein Rich yeast bun with jam filling

Bückling bloater, kipper

Bündnerfleisch cured, dried beef served in paper-thin
slices

European Menu Guide

Bunter Hans (speciality of Holstein and North Germany) a very large light breadcrumb dumpling, served with either stewed vegetables or stewed dried fruits

Büsumer Schnittchen slices of toast topped with eggs scrambled with onions and shrimps

Butter butter; *Kräuterbuter*, parsley butter; *Sardellenbutter*, anchovy butter

Buterknöpfe small 'buttons' of batter used to garnish clear soup

Butterkäse Austrian soft cheese, shaped like a loaf. It is unsalted and full-cream, and has a mild but slightly sour smell and taste

Butterkringel ('butter squiggles') very ligh butter biscuits, either ring-shaped or S-shaped

Buttermilch buttermilk; *Buttermilchsuppe*, buttermilk soup with eggs and chives

Butternockerlsuppe rich beef broth with small dumplings

Butterreis buttered rice

Cayennepfeffer cayenne pepper

Cervelatwurst spreadable, highly spiced, smoked pork and beef sausage

Champignon button mushroom

Chicorée endive, chicory

Cognac, Kognak cognac; *Cognac Plaumenpudding*, moulded pudding consisting of plum purée, lemon, brandy and cinnamon, garnished with cream and almonds

-creme pudding

Curryeis curried rice

Dampfnudeln small yeast pastry balls served with stewed fruit, jam or vanilla sauce

Datel date

Dorsch a variety of cod

Dresdner Dresden-style

Durchgebraten well-done (steak)

Edamer Austian cheese, made in Salzburg and the Steiermark; a copy of the Dutch Edam

Edelpilzkäse Austrian full-cream soft cheese, from the Steiermark, which has a distinctive sharp, slightly mouldy flavour

Ei Egg; *gekocht*, boiled; *weichgekocht*, soft-boiled;

wachsweichgekocht, soft-boiled; *hartgekocht*, hard-boiled; *panierte Eier*, soft-boiled eggs in a breadcrumb coating; *Rühreier*, scrambled eggs; *Spiegelei*, fried egg; *Verlorene Eier*, poached eggs; *Verlorene Eier Erzbischof* ('Archbishop'), poached eggs in chicken liver rings; *Verlorene Eier Farneser Art*, poached eggs in chicken liver rings; *Eigelb*, egg yolk; *Eiweiss*, egg white; *Eierkäse* ('egg cheese'), a sweet-savoury moulded pudding; *Eiernockerln*, eggs scrambled and fried with *Nockerln* (see below); *Nürnberger Eier*, hard-boiled eggs coated in batter and fried, served with a wine sauce

Eierapfel, Eierfrucht, Eierpflanze eggplant

Eierkuchen soufflé pancake

Eierstich firm egg custard, cut into strips, or diced, used as a garnish for soups

Einspänner black coffee topped with whipped cream

Eintopf Stew

Eis ice-cream; *Erdbeer-*, strawberry; *Karamel-*, caramel; *Mokka-*, coffee; *Schokoladen-*, chocolate; *vanille-*, vanilla; *Zitronen-*, lemon

Eisbein pickled pig's knuckle

Eiskaffee iced coffee, made with either ice cream or whipped cream

Emmenthaler Bavarian copy of the Swiss *Emmenthal* (*Gruyère*) cheese

Endive chicory, endive

Engelswurz angelica

Englisch rare (steak)

Ente duck; *Berliner Art*, roast duckling with apple and marjoram stuffing; *Gedämpfte Ente*, duck steamed with root vegetables and sage; *Vierländer Mastente* ('four countries'), roast duckling with stuffing made of apples, bread and blackberry brandy

Erbse pea; *erbsensuppe*, pea soup

Erdapfel (S.Germany) potato; *Erdapfelknödl* (Austrian), small potato dumplings with chives

Erdbeere strawberry; *Erdbeer Kaltschale*, chilled wild strawberry and white wine soup

Essig vinegar

Essiggurke gherkin

Essigkren prepared horseradsih

European Menu Guide

Estragon tarragon

Fadennudelm vermicelli

Falscher Hase ('false hare') meat loaf made of beef, veal and pork

Fasan pheasant, often stuffed with chestnut purée and cooked in buitter, or (in Austria) roasted in butter and basted with sour cream, served with braised red cabbage or sauerkraut; *Badische Art*, rubbed with brandy, lemon and thyme before roasting; *nach Buohmischer Art*, stuffed with cold roast snipe, mixed with herbs and truffles, and flambéed with brandy when cooked

Faschierter Braten pork and beef meat loaf, served with sour cream sauce

Faschiertes minced meat

Feige fig

Felchen (1) whitefish: (2) *Féra* (kind of salmon trout)

fenchel fennel

Filet (1) fillet; *Filetsteak*, beef steak; *Rindfilet*, fillet steak: (2) steak (fish)

Fisch fish; *Fischgericht*, fish dish; *Fischklösse*, fish dumplings; *Fischsuppe*, fish soup; *Gespickter Fisch*, whole fish baked with onions and vegetables; *Westerländer Fischsuppe*, hearty soup of fish, shell fish, bacon, vegetables and noodles

Fischbeuschelsuppe fish roe and vegetable soup

Fischmilcher soft roe

Fisolen French (green) beans

Flammeri flummery

Fleckerln very small, square noodles; *Fleckerlsuppe* (Austrian), strong beef broth garnished with *Fleckerln*; *Schinkenfleckerln*, noodles with sour cream and minced ham added

Fleisch meat; *Fleischbrühe*, clear beef broth, often garnished with tiny pancake strips, dumplings, or egg custard shapes; *Fleischklösse*, *Fleischknödel*, minced meat and herb dumplings; *Fleischkuchen*, pork, onion and potato mmeat loaf, served with onion sauce, potatoes and sauerkraut; *Fleischkäse*, type of Bologna sausage

Flohkrebs prawns

Flunder flounder

Flusskrebs crayfish (freshwater)

Forelle trout, usually cooked *au bleu* (see Blaufisch); *Gebackene Forelle Starnberger Art*, fried trout with shallot, lemon and herb sauce

Frankfurter Frankfurt-style; *Frankfurter Bettelmann* ('Beggar's apple pudding'), pudding made of rye bread soaked in cider, apples, raisins and cinnamon; *Frankfurter grüne Sauce*, mixed herb sauce; *Frankfurter Pudding*, light steamed pudding flavoured with almonds and cinnamon, served with a lemony red wine sauce; *Frankfurter Würstchen*, frankfurter sausage, usually served hot with sauerkraut or cold with potato salad

Fridatten strips of pancake used as a garnish for soups; *Fridattensuppe*, rich beef broth with pancake strips and chopped chives

Friesisch Friesland-style

Frikadellen croquettes

Frischling young wild boar, used to make pâté

Froschkeulen, Froschschenkel frogs' legs

Fruchtsaft fruit juice, squash

Fruchtspeise mixed fruit jelly

Frühlingssupe spring vegetable soup

Frühstückskäse ('breakfast cheese') fairly soft Limburger-type cheese made from whole or partly skimmed cow's-milk

Fürst Puckler-Rahmbombe iced bombe

Gans goose; *Gänseklein*, goose giblets; *Gänseleber*, goose liver; *Gänseleber Mit Äpfeln und Zwiebeln*, goose liver in breadcrumbs with apples and onion, sometimes served with a madeira and mushroom sauce; *Gänseleberpastete*, goose liver pâté (pâté de foie gras); *Gänselebertuffeln*, goose liver truffles; *Gänseschwarzsauer*, soup made from goose with vegetables, prunes and spices, thickened with goose blood; *Gänslsuppe*, thick goose soup; *Pommerscher Gänsebraten*, roast goose with prune, apple and rye bread stuffing; *Thüringer Gans*, roast goose with a stuffing of onion, apple, clove and marjoram

Garnele prawn

garnitur garnish

gebacken baked

European Menu Guide

gebraten (1) fried: (2) roasted

gedämpft steamed

gedünst poached

Geflügel poultry; *Geflügel Ragoût* (Austrian), stew made from giblets and leftover poultry with tomatoes, onion and herbs

Geflügelklein giblets; *Braunschweiger Geflügelklein*, chicken giblets and wings with sausage meat balls in a mushroom, asparagus and lemon sauce; *Geflügelkleinsuppe*, soup made from giblets and vegetables with parsley and sour cream

gefüllt stuffed

gegrillt grilled

gehackt diced

Gehirnwurst sausage made of pig's brains and pork with mace

gekocht boiled

gemischt mixed

Gemüse vegetables; *Gemischtes Gemüse*, mixed vegetables

Geräuchert smoked

G'röstl, Geröstel, Tiroler G'röstl (Austrian) hash of fried onion rings and potatoes with sliced cooked beef and caraway seeds

Gerste barley; *Gerstensuppe*, beef or mutton broth with barley

geschmort braised, smothered (e.g. chops)

Geschnetzelt meat cut into strips stewed in wine to produce a thick sauce

geschwenkt sautéed

Geselchtes (S.German and Austrian) cured or smoked pork

Girardirostbraten (Austrian) Girardi steak served with whitye wine and sour cream sauce

Götterspeise dessert of chantilly cream mixed with grated pumpernickel and chocolate

Griess semolina; *Griessklösse*, *Griessknödl*, semolina dumplings; *Bayerische Griessklösse*, semolina dumplings with shallots and parsley; *Griessnockerlsuppe*, semolina-dumpling soup; *Griesschmarrn* (Austrian), semolina milk pudding with raisins; *Griesswürfel*, garnish for soups made from cold mixture of semolina and seasoned chicken or veal stock

grün green

Grützwurst see *Pinkelwurst*

Gugelhupf, Guglhupf traditional Austrian yeastcake of which there are many varieties, most of which contain almonds and raisins; *Marmorguglhupf*, chocolate and vanilla marble cake; *Rahmguglhupf, Gugelhupf* with cream

Gulasch fairly spicy meat or poultry stew, with sour cream added when veal is used, served with *Nockerln* (see below); *Gulaschsuppe*, spiced soup of stewed beef

Gurke cucumber; *Gefüllte Gurke*, cucumber with minced meat and dill stuffing, wrapped in bacon and casseroled in stock; *Hannoversches Gurkengemüse*, cucumbers braised with onion and tomatoes in lemon juice and dill weed, to which sour cream is added

Hackbraten meatloaf

Haferflocken oats; *Haferbrei, Hafergrütze*, porridge; *Salziger Haferkeks*, oatcake

Hagebutte rosehip; *Hagebuttenmarmelade*, rosehip preserve; *Hagebuttensuppe*, rosehip soup, made with white wine, lemon, cinnamon and cloves

Hähnchen chicken; *Berliner Art*, roast chicken with rice, onion, celery, grape, almond and thyme stuffing

Hamburger Hamburg-style; *Hamburger Kasserolle*, casserole of fish and shellfish with artichokes and mushrooms cooked in mushroom and white wine sauce; *Hamburger Rundstück*, open sandwich of lettuce topped with cold roast pork or veal, with mayonnaise, yoghurt and herb sauce

Hammel mutton; *Hammelbrust*, breast of lamb; *Hammelkeule als Wildbret*, leg of mutton cooked like venison; *Hammelripe*, mutton cutlet; *Hammelschulter*, shoulder of mutton, often braised with onion and cucumber; *Hammelwürste*, dish consisting of mutton sausages, fat pork and herbs and spices; *Hammelzungen*, sheep's tongue; *Westfälische Hammelkeule*, roast leg of lamb in a yoghurt and vegetable coating

Hanoversch Hanover-style

Hase hare; *Hasenbraten*, young hare cooked in red wine with vegetables and herbs, with sour cream and hare's blood added; *Hasenbraten in Bier*, oatmeal-coated hare joints cooked in light beer; *Hasenpfeffer*, jugged hare; *Hasenrücken mit Meerrettich*, saddle of hare in horseradish sauce; *Schleisischer Hasenbraten*, hare or rabbit coated with nutmeg and thyme seasoned flour, fried with pimiento and served with crisp bacon and sour cream gravy

Haselhuhn hazel grouse

Haselnuss hazelnut

Hauptelsalat (Austrian) brawn

Hecht pike

Hefekranz ring-shaped coffee cake

Heidelbeere bilberry, blueberry

Helibutt halibut

heiss hot; *Heisser Seehund* ('hot seal') hot punch consisting of white wine and brandy with raisins, flavoured with lemon and cinnamon

Hendl chicken

Hering herring; *Bismarckhering*, soused herring with onions; *Bratheringe*, soused herrings; *Gebratene Heringe*, heavily salted herrings, marinated then fried in egg and breadcrumb coating; *Heringe in Weinsauce*, herrings baked in white wine; *Matjesfilet nach Hausfrauenart* ('home-made-style'), fillets of herring with apples and onions; *Matjeshering*, salted young herrings; *Pikante Heringe*, fresh herrings with roes in white wine, onion, garlic and herb sauce

Herz heart

Herzmuschel cockle

Himbeere raspberry

Himmel und Erde ('heaven and earth') mashed potatoes mixed with lemony apple sauce, bacon and onions

Hirn brains; *Hirnpofesen* (Austrian), fried sandwich with a filling of calf's brain, onion, parsley and egg, served with spinach; *Hirnschoberlsuppe* (Austrian), brain soup

Holstein, Holsteiner Art Holstein-style

Holunderbeere elderberry; *Holundersuppe*, elderberry soup

Honig honey; *Honigkuchen*, honey biscuits; *Honigwabe*, honeycomb

Honigmelone honeydew melon

Hopfen hops; *hopfenkeime*, hops with mushrooms;

Hopfensalat, salad made with young hop buds, cooked like asparagus and served either cold with lemon juice and mayonnaise or hot with melted butter

Hoppel-Poppel scrambled eggs with diced sausages or bacon

Huhn chicken; *Berliner Hühnerfrikassee*, chicken with ham, sausages, mushrooms, capers and asparagus spears in a white wine, lemon and sour cream sauce; *Böhmisches Huhn*, roast chicken with vermicelli, parsley and cheese stuffing; *Huhn mit Reis*, *Hühnchen in weisser Sauce*, chicken joints in white sauce served with rice; *Huhn nach Bauernart*, chicken joints fried in a cheesy breadcrumb coating served with a mushroom sauce; *Huhn nach Jägerart*, fried chicken joints served in a tomato-flavoured sauce of mushrooms and shallots in brandy; *Huhnerbraten*, roast chicken with an onion and mushroom stuffing; *Hühnerbrühe*, chicken broth; *Hühnerbrühe mit Nudeln*, chicken noodle soup; *Hühnerleber*, chicken liver; *Huhnerleberpastete*, chicken liver pâté, *Paprikahuhn*, chicken cooked in a paprika and sour cream sauce; *Sacher Huhn* (an Austrian dish named after its creator, Madame Sacher, owner of the Hotel Sacher in Vienna), young chicken stuffed with sausage-meat, goose liver and sweetbreads, cooked in madeira; *Saures Huhn*, chicken cooked in a sour cream sauce

Hummer lobster; *Hummer in Weissbier*, lobster served with a sauce made with light beer and shallots, and caraway seeds

Husarenfilet (Austrian) fillet steak larded with ham and strips of gherkin, cooked in a thin cream sauce; *Husarenfilet-Fleisch*, small, thin, beaten slices of pork, veal and fillet steak cooked in a sour cream sauce

Hutzelbrot spicy fruit loaf

Ingwer ginger

Innereien offal

Jägerart, nach hunter's-style: sautéed with mushrooms and root vegetables, served in wine gravy

Jagerpunch ('hunter's punch') hot punch of wine, rum and tea flavoured with lemon spices

Jägersuppe ('hunter's soup') hearty soup of partridge, ham, vegetables adn wine

Jägerwurst ('hunter's sausage') very hard, flat smoked sausage of paprika-flavoured pork

Jacobsmuschein scallops

Joghurt yoghurt

Johannisbeeren currants

Jorbkäse sour milk cheese

Jungfernbraten (Austrian) pork fillet braised with onions and carrots, and sour cream

Jungschweinskaree (Austrian) roast pork, rubbed with crushed caraway seeds

Kabeljau cod; *in Biersauce*, cod baked in brown ale, with gingerbread, onion and shallot, and served in the strained and thickened sauce; *nach Hamburger Art*, cod cooked in wine, served in an oyster sauce

Kaffee coffee; *Eiskaffee*, iced coffee; *Espresso*, expresso; *Koffeinfreien Kaffee*, caffeine-free coffee; *Milchkaffee*, coffee with milk; *mit Sahne*, with cream; *Mokka*, mocca; *Schwarzen Kaffee*, black coffee

Kaiserfleisch (Austrian) smoked pickled pork with sauerkraut and dumplings, or split green pea purée

Kaiserschmarren (Austrian) shredded pancake with raisins served with syrup

Kaiserschnitzel (Austrian) veal cutlet braised in stock and sour cream sauce

Kakao cocoa

Kalb, Kalbfleisch veal; *Kalbsbrust*, breast of veal; *Kalbskeule*, leg of veal; *Kalbsleber*, calf's liver; *Kalbsnierenbraten*, roast loin of veal; *Kalbsrippe*, veal cutlets with *Kümmelsauce* (see below); *Kalbszunge*, calf's tongue; *Gefüllter Kalbsbraten*, leg of veal with onion, kidney and anchovy stuffing, served with hot sour cream; *Gefüllte Kalbsbrust nach Wiener Art*, Viennese stuffed breast of veal; *Kalb Holstein*, fried veal cutlets in breadcrumbs, topped with a poached egg and various garnishes

kalt cold

Kaltschale, Kalte Obstsuppe fruit soup, served chilled, sometimes containing beer or wine

Kaninchen rabbit; *Schwäbische Kaninchenpastete*, rabbit pâté in puff pastry

Kapaun capon

Kapern capers

Kapuziner nasturtum leaves, frequently used in salads

Karfiol (Austrian) cauliflower

Kärntner Nudeln oval-shaped noodles filled with dried fruit, sugar, cinnamon and cream-soaked breadcrumbs

Karotten small carrots

Karpfen carp; *Gebackener Karpfen* (traditional Christmas Eve fare in North Germany and Austria), fillets fried in breadcrumbs

Kartoffel potato; *kartoffelbälle*, potato balls; *Kartofelbrei*, mashed potatoes; *Kartoffelklösse*, *Kartoffelknödel*, potato dumplings; *Kartofelkroketten*, potato croquettes, *Kartoffelpuffer*, potato fritters, pancakes; *Kartoffelsalat*, potato salad; *Pellkartoffeln*, potatoes boiled in their jackets; *Petersilienkartoffeln*, parsleyed potatoes; *Salzkartoffeln*, boiled potatoes; *Westfälische Kartoffeln*, mashed potatoes mixed with apple purée, grilled with a breadcrumb topping

Käse cheese; *Frischkäse*, 'fresh', soft cheese to be eaten within a few days of being made; *Hartkäse*, firm cheese, hard enough to be cut into slices; *Käsebrett*, cheese board; *Käseteller*, plate of mixed cheeses

Käsehäppchen cheese sticks

Käsekuchen cheesecake

Käsesalat strong cheese sprinkled with caraway seeds, served with a vinaigrette sauce

Käsestrudel (Austrian) very thin layers of pastry with a cream cheese and sultana filling

Kasseler lightly smoked pork tenderloin, usually served with sauerkraut; *Kasserler Rippenspeer*, smoked pork spare rib

Kastanie chestnut; *Kastanientorte*, chestnut cake

kaviar caviar

Kerbel chervil

keule leg, haunch

Kirsche cherry; *Hamburger Kirschkaltschale*, cold cherry soup flavoured with cinnamon; *Kirschstrudel*, cherry strudel; *Sauerkirsche*, sour cherry; *Westfälischer Kirschkuchen*, cherry fruit cake

Klopse meatballs; *Königsberger Klopse*, poached meatballs with lemon sauce, sometimes with capers added

European Menu Guide

Klösschen meatballs

Klösse, Knödel very light dumplings, found in various forms, mainly as a garnish for soups; *Wiener Knödelsuppe*, rich beef broth with dumplings

Knackwürste, Knockwürste smoked pork and beefy spicy sausages

Knoblauch garlic; *Knoblauchbrot*, garlic bread; *Knoblauchwurst*, beef and pork sausage containing large pieces of fat and garlic

Knöderl, Knödel small dumplings mainly used in soups; *Tiroler Knodlsuppe*, rich beef broth with large bread and salt pork dumplings

Koch (Austrian) (1) pudding; *Wienerkoch*, soufflé pudding; (2) purée

Kohl cabbage; *Gefüllte Kohlwürstchen*, cabbage leaves stuffed with minced meat and onion, cooked in white wine

Kohlrabi kohl rabi (a turnip-like vegetable of which both leaves and root are eaten)

Kohlroulade cabbage leaves stuffed with minced meat

Kokosnuss coconut

Kimpott stewed fruit, compote

Königinpastete puff pastry shell filled with diced meat and mushrooms

Königinsuppe meat soup with sour cream and almonds, served with small semolina or bone marrow dumplings

Königsberger Königsberg-style

Königswurst ('King's, or 'royal' sausage) sausage made from chicken and partridge, with truffle and mushroom and Rhenish wine

Kopfsalat lettuce

kotelett cutlet, chop

Köthener Schusterpfanne ('shoemaker's pot') loin of pork seasoned with herbs, pot-roasted with potatoes and pears

Krabbe prawn, shrimp

Kraftbrühe consommé; *Kraftbrühe mit Ei*, beef consommé with raw egg

Krambambuli hot rum and red wine punch

Krapfen small pastry, either a doughnut or a meat-filled pastry; *Wiener Krapfen*, lemon-flavoured doughnuts

Krapferln profiteroles

Kraut (1) cabbage; *Bayrisches Kraut*, cabbage braised with bacon and caraway seeds in white wine; *Rothenburger Kraubraten*, cabbage and bacon baked with potatoes and a herby beef mixture in savoury custard sauce; (2) herb (*Kräuter Herbs*); *Kräuterbutter*, herb butter; *Kräuterkäsw*, parsley cheese; *Kräutermischung*, bouquet garni

Krebs (1) crabs; (2) crayfish; *krebssuppe*, traditional crayfish soup from Hamburg

Kren horseradish; *Krenfleisch*, pork, usually brawn, served with shredded vegetables and horseradish

Kuchen cake

Küken chicken (young); *Bremer Kükenragout*, chicken stewed with shrimps, asparagus, peas and mushrooms with sour cream added to the sauce

Kümmel caraway seed; *Kümmelkäse*, caraway cheese; *Kümmelsauce*, sauce made with sour cream, paprika and caraway seeds, served with veal; *Kummelstangen*, cheese straws with caraway seeds

Kurbis (1) marrow; *Kurbiskraut* (Austrian), marrow cooked in a thick onion, herb and sour cream sauce; (2) pummpkin

Kutteln tripe

Labskaus hash of potatoes, onions and either fish or meat

Lachs salmon

Lamm, Lammfleisch lamb

Langusten spiny lobster

Lappenpickert potato cake, made with sour cream

lauch leek

leber liver; *Berliner Leber*, liver with onion and apples; *Leberkäse*, meat loat; *Leberknödel*, liver dumplings with bacon, onion, and herbs; *Leberknödelsuppe*, liver dumpling soup; *Lebernockerln*, small liver dumplings; *Leberwurst*, liver sausage; *Tiroler Leber*, liver and onions in a sour cream and caper sauce

Lebkuchen small cakes of honey, spices, nuts and candied peel, often baked in elaborate moulds and traditionally eaten at Christmas; *Nürnverger Lebkuchen*, similar to *Lebkuchen*, but with the cake mixture spread on wafers prior to baking, then iced

European Menu Guide

Leckerli ginger snaps

Leipziger Leipzig-style; *Leipziger Allerlei* ('a little of everything'), thick beef stock stew with mixed vegetables, garnished with hard-boiled eggs

Likör (1) cordial; (2) liqueur

Limburger Käse (1) (Austrian) sharp cheese made with either full or three-quarter cream, covered in a red wax coating; (2) (German) soft delicate cheese

Limonade lemonade

Linse lentil; *Berlincer Linsentopf*, lentils stewed with potatoes and bacon, served with onions and parsley; *Linsensuppe*, lentle soup

Linzer Torte (Austrian) rich almond and raspberry jam tart

Liptauer, Liptai flavoured sour milk cheese

Mainze Handkase (Austrian) sharp sour milk cheese

Mainzer Käse (German) sour milk soft cheese

Mais (1) maize (corn); (2) sweetcorn

Marjoran marjoram

Makkaroni macaroini

Makrele mackerel

Makrone macaroon; *Makronentorte*, macaroon tart

Mandarine tangarine

Mandel almond; *Mandelkren* (Austrian) cold or hot almond and horseradish sauce

Mandelmilch almond milk

Marielle apricot; *Marillenstrudel* (Austrian), apricot *Strudel*

Marinebraten (Austrian) braised fillet steak in a cream and vegetable sauce

mariniert marinated

markknödlsuppe (Austrian) beef marrow dumpling soup

Marmelade jam; *Orangemarmelade*, marmelade

Marmorkuchen marble cake

Marone chestnut

Marzipanmasse almond paste

Masthuhn, Masthühnchen pullet chicken; *Masthuhn nach Bauernart*, pullets fried in a cheese and breadcrumb coating, served in a white wine and mushroom sauce

Matjesheringe young, salted herrings, eaten particularly in the Bremerhaven area where the majority are caught

Matrosen-Bröte ('sailor's sandwich') seasoned egg mixture on rye bread, garnished with anchovies and gherkins

Maultaschen Spinach-filled ravioli, traditionally eaten on Good Friday in Wurttemburg

Meeresfruchte seafood

Meerrettich horseradish

Mehlnockerln tiny flour dumplings

Mecklenvurger Bratwurst pork sausage from Mecklenburg, flavoured with allspice

Melange coffee and hot milk topped with whipped cream

Melone melon (cantaloupe)

Mewwwurst spreading sausage made from pork and spices

Milch milk; *kalte Milch*, cold milk; *warme Milch*, hot milk; *Milchmixgetränk*, milkshake

Milchrahmstrudel *studel* with sour cream, eggs and sultana filling

Mineralwasser mineral water

Mirabelle mirabelle, a small, yellow plum

Mischlingskäse (Austrian) sharp, hard cheese

mittel medium

Mohntorte poppy seed cake

Mohrenkopf chocolate meringue with whipped-cream filling

Mohrle im hemd ('dark maidens in skirts') cold dessert consisting of rum-soaked sponge finger biscuits layered with a chocolate sauce

Möhre, Mohrrübe carrot

Mondbohne butterbean

Mondseer Schlosskäse (Austrian) small full-cream Limburger-type cheese

Münchner Munich-style

Mürbeteig rich shortcrust pastry

Muschel mussel; *Muschelsuppe*, mussel chowder

Napfkuchen ring-shaped fruit cake

Neger (Austrian) stong black coffee

Neunauge lemprey eel

Nieheimer Hopfenkäse sour milk cheese from Nieheim, Westphalia, cured and packed with hops

Niere kidney; *Nieren Stuttgarter Art*, sautéed kidneys in white wine and cream sauce with onion, lemon and herbs and spices; *Nierenknödel*, small kidney dumplings

European Menu Guide

Nudeln noodles; *Nudelsuppe*, noodle soup

Nürnberger Nuremberg-style; *Nürnberger Wurst*, sausage made from pork and bacon flavoured with kirsch and seasoned with herbs and spices

Nuss nut; *Gemischte Nüsse*, assorted nuts; *Nussgebäck*, nut, chocolate and ginger biscuits traditionally eaten on New Year's Eve; *Nussstrudel*, *Strudel* with hazelnut filling; *Nusstorte*, rum and walnut cake

Nussschwarzer (Austrian) stong black coffee

Oberskren (Austrian) cream and horseradish sauce

Obst fruit; *Obstsalat*, fruit cocktail; *Obstsuppe*, fruit soup

Ochsenfleisch beef; *Ochsenschwanz*, oxtail; *Weimarer Ochsenzunge*, tongue with raisin sauce

Öl oil; *Olivenöl*, olive oil

Oliven olives

Omelett omelette

Orangeade orangeade

orangenmarmelade marmalade

Ostpreussisch East Prussian

Palatschinken pancakes, usually filled with jam, cheese, sausages or nuts, and topped with hot chocolate sauce and nuts

Pamplemuse grapefruit

Pannfisch large fishcake

Paprika Paradeiser (Austrian) tomato pastete

Pâté Pfalzer Rhineland-style

Pfannfisch cod; *Friesischer Pfannfisch*, cod served in lemon sauce with cubed potatoes

Pfannkuchen (1) pancake; *Pfalzer Pfannkuchen-Auflauf*, pancakes filled with spinach, in a cheese sauce; (2) doughnut; *Berliner Pfannkuchen*, jam doughnut, traditionally eaten on New Year's Eve; (3) (Austrian) apricot pastry in rum syrup

Pfeffer pepper; *Pfefferkuchen*, spiced 'pepper' cake

Pfeffer-Potthast ('pepperpot') stew of beef, onions and herbs, strongly seasoned with pepper

Pfifferling chanterelle mushroom

Pfirsich peach

Pfirsich-bowle peaches in brandy and wine, with club soda

Pflaume plum; *Cognac Pflaumenpudding*, moulded pudding

of plum purée and brandy, garnished with cream and almonds; *Pflaumenkuchen*, plum tart; *Pflaumenmus*, plum jam

Pichelsteiner (Eintopf) meat and vegetable stew

pikant piquant

Pilz mushroom

Pinkelwurst smoked spicy pork sausage from Bremen; in othe parts of Germany known as *Grützwurst*

Pofesen Austrian version of *Arme ritter* (see above)

Pökel (1) brine; (2) pickle

Pökelfleisch (1) salt meat; (2) brawn

Pommersch Pomeranian-style; *Pommersche Suppe*, soup made with haricot beans, celery and onion

Pommes frites chips, french fries

Poree leek

Prebkohlsuppe (Austrian) beef broth with stuffed cabbage

Prieselbeere cranberry

Pretzel savoury biscuit, shaped like a loose knot and sprinkled with coarse salt and cumin seed

Printen honey biscuits

Pumpernickel heavy black rye bread from Westphalia - purée creamed (vegetables)

Pute, Puter turkey; *Festlicher Putenbraten* ('festive'), roast stuffed turkey

Quargel, Quargelkäse (Austrian) sharp, sour milk cheese

Quark cottage cheese; *Quarkklösse*, cottage cheese dumplings; *Quarkkoch*, cheesecake mould, sometimes served with lemmon sauce; *Quarktorte*, cold cottage cheese, lemon and cinnamon tart

Quitte quince

Radieschen radish

Rahm cream

Rahmkäse (Austrian) salted, slightly sour cream cheese, found almost exclusively in rural areas

Räucheraal smoked eel

Räucherhering smoked herring

Rauchfleisch smoked beef; *Hamburger Rauchfleisch*, boiled smoked brisket served with horseradish

Rebhuhn partridge, usually roasted with juniper berries and served with sauerkraut; *Rebhuhn auf Wiener Art*, cooked in a parcel of cabbage leaves and served in a sour cream sauce

Regensburger Regensburg-style; *Regensburger Braten*, pork and beef meat loaf; *Regensburgher Wurst*, spicy, moist sausage from Regensburg (lower Bavaria)

Reh roe deer, considered to be the finest form of venison; *Baden-Badener Reh*, roast saddle of roe deer served with compote of pears and redcurrant jelly; *Rehpastete*, venison meat loaf; *Rehrücken*, saddle or haunch of roe deer or vension

Rehrücken (Austrian) oblong chocolate cake with chocolate icing spiked with blanched almonds, in imitation of a haunch of venison

Reindlbiftek (Austrian) braised fillet steak, served with fried egg, fried potatoes and gherkins

Reineclaude, Reneklode greengage

Reis rice; *Reisklösse*, small veal or chicken and rice dumplings; *Reiswürstchen* ('rice sausages') (Austrian) mixture of veal, rice and eggs wrapped in rice paper, coated in egg and breadcrumbs and fried; used to garnish soups

Rhabarber rhubarb

Rheinisch Rhine-style; *Rheinischer Weihnachtssalat* ('Christmas salad') potatoes, apples, onion, veal, ham, pickles, herring and walnuts, in a mayonnaise and sour cream sauce; *Rheinsalm*, salmon cooked in a white wine and cream sauce

Rinderhirn ox brains, fried in egg and breadcrumb coating

Rinderschmorbraten braised steak

Rindfleisch beef; *Rindfleischwurst*, beef and pork sausage

Rindsrouladen beef rolls, stuffed with bacon and onion, braised with vegetables

Rippchen pork chop or cutlet

Rippensteak rib steak

Rochen skate, ray

roh (1) raw; (2) rare (meat)

Rollmops fresh herring rolls filled with onion, gherkin and peppercorn and marinated in spiced vinegar

Romadur Käse (Austrian and Bavarian) mild soft-ripened ccow's milk cheese

Rosenkohl brussels sprouts

Rostbraten (1) roast beef (normally well-done); (2) (in Austria) fried thick sirloin steak

Rösti hashed-brown potatoes

rot red

Rotbarsch red sea-bass

Rote Beete, Rote Ruben beetroot

Rote Grütze (1) thickened purée of raspberries and redcurrants cooked in red wine; (2) red berry cream; (3) red berry jelly

Rothenburger Rothenburg-style

Rotkohl red cabbage; *auf Bayrische Art*, red cabbage cooked in white wine and vinegar with raisins, boiled bacon and caraway seeds; *auf Berliner Art*, simmered with apple, onion, cloves, vinegar and red wine; *auf Westfälische Art*, similar to the Berlin version but with fried onnion and a ham bone added, and sprinkled with vinegar before serving

Roulade stuffed beef or veal roll, braised

Russische Eier hard-boiled eggs with mayonnaise

Saarländer Saarland-style; *Saarländer Becher* ('goblet'), grapes served hot or cold in a white wine and egg custard

Sachertorte (Austrian, named after its creator, Franz Sacher, pastry-chef to Prince Metternich and founder of the Hotel Sacher in Vienna) rich chocolate and apricot cake, served with cream

Sahne cream; *saure Sahne*, sour cream

Saibling char

Salamikäse (Austrian) slightly sour full cream cheese shaped like a salami sausage

Salat salad; *Bremer Salat*, salad of pickled herring, luncheon meat, apple and celery in a sour cream, curry and mayonnaise sauce; *Süddeutscher Salat*, onion, parsley, chives and mustard salad dressing

Salm salmon; *Rheinsalm*, salmon cooked in a white wine and cream sauce

Salz salt

Salzburger Nockerln (Austrian) rich sweet dumplings, served as a pudding

Salzgurke gherkin

Sandtorte ('sand cake') a very dry and crumbly cake,

European Menu Guide

flavoured with rum

Sandwich sandwich

Sardelle anchovy; *Sardellenkäse*, anchovy cheese

Sardinen sardines

Sauce sauce

Sauer sour (fruit etc); *säuerlich*, sour (wine, vinegar)

Sauerampfer sorrel

Sauerbraten braised beef (marinated in vinegar);
Rhenischer Sauerbraten, beef marinated and braised in
spiced vinegar and vegetables, served with raisin and sour
ccream sauce and mixed dried fruit

Sauerkraut sauerkraut (cabbage, salted and shredded,
fermented to give it the slightly sour taste which gives it its
name). Often braised with onion, bacon, apples and
potato

scheibchen thin slice, sliver (of meat etc.)

Schellfisch haddock; *nach Hamburger Art*, haddock layered
with potatoes and onions, baked in a cream sauce

Schiffchen ('boats') small pastry boats with various fillings;
Admirals Art, shrimp; *Gräfin Landi*, onion soufflé; *Indische*,
curry; *Russische*, onion and caviar

Schildkrotensuppe turtle soup

Schinken (1) ham; (2) (boiled and smoked) gammon;
gekochter Schinken, boiled ham; *roher Schinken*, cured ham;
Schinkenbrötchen, ham roll; *Schinkenspeck*, bacon;
Schinkenwurst, ham sausage; *Schinkenbegräbnis*, ('buried
ham'), ham and cheese macaroni; *Schinckenfleckerln*,
noodles with sour cream and minced ham;
Schinkenröllchen mit Spargel, rolled ham with asparagus
filling; *auf Mecklenburger Art*, skinned boiled ham baked in a
spiced rye breadcrumb coating; *auf Schwäbischer Art*,
braised in beer and stock with onions; *mit Bohnen und
Birnen* (Westphalian), sliced raw ham cooked with
vegetables and fruit

Schlachtplatte platter of various sausages and cold meats

Schlag, Schlagober Viennese term for whipped cream,
flavoured with vanilla sugar; also called *Wiener Schlagobers*

Schleie tench

Schlesischer Silesian-style; *Schlesisches Himmelreich*,
('Silesian heaven'), pork chops with fruit and dumplings

Schlosserbuben (Austrian) battered prunes stuffed with almonds and sprinkled with grated chocolate

Schlosskäse (Austrian) very small cheese, shaped like a miniature sandcastle (hence its name, 'castle cheese')

Schmalzgebackenes, Beignet fritter

Schmarrn ('a mere nothing') a traditional Austrian dish consisting of shredded pancakes, made with semolina (*Griessschmarrn*), flour (*Kaiserschmarrn*), croissants (*Kipfelschmarrn*) or bread (*Semmelschmarrn*)

Schmorbraten pot-roast

Schmortopf, Kasserole casserole

Schnecken (1) snails; (2) (Austrian) puff pastries with raisin, walnut and chocolate filling, rolled up like a swiss roll then baked in slices, resembling snails

Schneeklösschen ('snow dumplings') meringue dumplings

Schnepfe snipe

Schnitte sandwich, sometimes open

Schnittkäse collective name for Austrian and German semi-hard cheeses

Schnittlauch chives

Schnitzel cutlet, escalope, usually of veal; *Bismarck Schnitzel*, fried in egg and breadcrumbs, garnished with plover's eggs, mushrooms, truffles and fresh tomato sauce; *Holsteiner Schnitzel*, fried in egg and breadcrumbs, garnished with poached egg, gherkins, beetroot, capers, anchovies, olives, lemon and parsley; *Kaiserschnitzel* (Austrian), braised in veal stock and sour cream sauce; *Leipziger Schnitzel*, fried in egg and breadcrumbs, served with *sauce béarnaise* and *Leipziger Allerlei* (see above); *Naturschnitzel*, coated in flour, fried in butter; *Paprika Schnitzel* (Austrian), fried with onions and paprika, served in sour cream gravy; *Paradies Schnitzel*, braised in tomato sauce, served wtih noodles or rice; *Pariser Schnitzel*, fried in egg and milk coating; *Rahmschnitzel*, served in a spicy cream sauce; *Schwäbisches Schnitzel*, fried in butter, lemon juice and cream, served with breadcrumb coated *Spätzle* (see below); *Wiener Schnitzel* (Austrian), thin escalopes fried in egg and breadcrumbs, garnished with lemon and parsley; *Zigeuner Schnitzel*, cooked in fresh tomato sauce with mushrooms and smoked ox tongue

European Menu Guide

Schokolade chocolate

scholle plaice

Schusterpfanne ('shoemaker's pot') stew of pork with
vegetables and pears

Schwäbisch Swabian-style; *Schwäbische Würste*, garlic pork
sausages, smoked or plain; *Schwäbischer Schlachtbraten*,
fillet of beef roasted and served in a vegetable and white
wine gravy

Schwammerlsauce (Austrian) mushroom sauce

Schwarz black

Schwarzbrot ('black bread') see *Pumpernickel*

Schwarze Johanisbeere blackcurrant

Schwarzfisch (Austrian) fish in spiced beer, with crumbled
honey cake, butter, redcurrant jelly or plum jam, dried
fruits and nuts

Schwarzwürste ('black sausages') spicy pork sausages

Schwarzwurzeln salsify

Schweinefleisch pork; *Schweinebraten*, roast pork

Schweinefleischkäse pork loaf

Schweinskarree cured and smoked pork fillet

Schweinskotelett pork cutlet, chop; *auf Berliner Art*, fried
in egg and breadcrumbs, garnished with apples, sauté
potatoes and red cabbage

Schweinsohren pig's ears

Schweinesulz (Austrian) pork cooked with vegetables,
herbs and wine vinegar; the meat is then sliced and set
with slices of hard-boiled egg in its own jelly

Schweizer Kraut marigold leaves

Seebarsch sea-bass

Seebutt brill

Seezunge lemon sole

Sellerie celery

Semmel roll; *Bayrische Semmelknödel*, bread dumplings
flavoured with onions and parsley; *Semmelklosse*, bread
dumplings with alomd and raisins; *Semmelknödel mit Pilzen*,
bread dumplings with mushrooms

Semmelkren horseradish and bread sauce

senf mustard

Serbisch Serbian-style

Serviettenknödel a single large semolina and cream

cheese dumpling

Spaghetti spaghetti

Spanferkel suckling pig

Spargel asparagus; *Spargelspitzen*, asparagus tips

Spargelkohl broccoli

Spätzle (S. German) (1) thick noodles; (2) dumplings;
Schwäbische Spätzle, tiny dumplings

Speck bacon; *Speckknödel*, bread dumplings with bacon

Spekulatius almond biscuits

Spickgans breast of goose, cured and smoked

Spinat spinach

Spitzkäse spiced sour milk cheese

Sprotten sprats

Sprudel sodawater

Stachelbeere gooseberry

Stangenkase, Bierkäse (Austrian) soft cream cheese
made with sour milk in Salzburg and the Steiermark

Stangenspargel asparagus spears

Starnberger Starnberg-style

Steak steak (meat)

Steinbutt turbot

Steirisches Wurzelfleisch (Styrian) casseroled pork and
vegetables

Stint smelt

Stollen yeast loaf filled with fruit and almonds, traditionally
eaten at Christmas (*Weihnachtsstollen*) and other holiday
times

Stör sturgeon

Stammer Max highly spiced minced pork served with eggs
and onions

Streichwurst spreading sausage

Streuselkuchen crumble cake

Strudel (Austrian) paper-thin pastry which can contain many
kinds of filling, the most popular being apple, cherry and
curd cheese

Stuttgarter Stuttgart-style

Sulperknochen (traditional dish from Hesse) boiled pickled
pork served with sauerkraut and pease pudding

Sülze brawn

Suppe soup; soups are very popular in Germany and

Austria, forming an essential part of the lunch-time meal

Süsssauer sweet-and-sour

Tafelspitz (Austrian) boiled beef served with hot/cold chive sauce

Tartaren-Bröte raw minced meat with an egg yolk on buttered rye bread, sprinkled with grated horesradish

Taube pigeon, squab

Tee Tea; *mit Milch*, with milk; *mit Zitrone*, with lemon; *Apfeltee*, apple tea; *Baldriantee*, Valerian tea; *Brennesseltee*, nettle tea; *Eistee*, iced tea; *Lindenblutentee*, lime tea; *Pfefferminztee*, peppermint tea

Teewurst very fine smoked pork sausage, for spreading

Teigwaren noodles

Thunfisch tunny, tuna

Thüringer Thuringian-style

Tilsiter Käse semi-hard cow's milk cheese, wtih flavour ranging from mild to moderately sharp

Tiroler Tyolean-style

Toast toast

Tomate tomato; *Tomatenketchup*, tomato ketchup; *Tomatensuppe*, tomato soup

Tomeri (Austrian) savoury pancake, with onions

Topfen- a prefix indicating the use of curd or cottage cheese in the dish; *Topfengolatschen* (Austrian), puff pastries with cottage cheese and fruit filling; *Topfenknödel* (Austrian), cottage cheese and breadcrumb dumplings; *Topfentorte* (Austrian), baked cheesecake topped with raisins; T*opfenpalaschinken*, curd pancake

Torte (1) layer cake; (2) tart or flan; *Törtchen*, tartlet

Toska-Törtchen (Austrian) ('Tosca tarts') chicken and cheese soufflé tarts

Traube grape

Trüffel truffle

Truthahn turkey

Ulmer Gerstlsuppe (Austrian) beef broth and barley soup

Wachtel quail; *auf Berliner Art*, quail with goose liver forcemeat stuffing, cooked in veal stock and served on an artichoke bottom, with *sauce allemande* and grated truffle

Waldmeister woodruff

Walnuss walnut

Warmbier hot beer soup

Wasser water; *Eiswasser*, iced warer

Wassermelone watermelon

Weichkäse cream cheese

Weichseltorte (Austrian) morello cherry tart

Weihnachts- Christmas

Weimarer Weimar-style

Wein wine; *Glühwein*, mulled wine

Weinbrand brandy

Weintraube grape

Weiss white

Weisse Rube turnip

Weissfisch dace

Weisskohl cabbage (white); *Westfälischer Weisskohl*, white cabbage with onion, apple and potato

Weisslackerkäse soft ripened cow's-milk cheese, from Bavaria

WeisswUurste ('white sausages') light, delicate pork and veal sausages from the Munich area

Weizen wheat; *Weizenbrot*, wheaten bread

Westfälisch Westphalian-style

Westerländer Westerland-style

Wiener Vienna-style, Viennese; *Wiener Wurst*, small frankfurter type of sausage

Wild game

Wildente wild duck

Wildschwein wild boar; *Falscher Wildschweinbraten* ('fake wild boar'), pork rubbed with juniper berries braised in red wine and served in a wine and cream sauce

Wilstermarschkäse semi-hard cow's-milk cheese, slightly acidic, from Schleswig-Holstein

Windbeutel cream puff

Wurst sausage; *Wurstplatte*, assorted cold cuts; *Wurstsalat*, sausage and onion salad

Würze seasoning, spices

Zander giant perch, pike-perch

Zichorie chicory

Zigeunernudeln ('gipsy noodles') puréed plums and noodles

Zimit cinnamon; *Zimtsterne*, star-shaped cinnamon biscuits

European Menu Guide

Zitrone lemon; *Zitronensaft*, lemon squash; *Zitronensirup*, lemon squash (undiluted); *Zitronentee*, lemon tea

Zucker sugar

Zuckermelone honeydew melon

Zunge tongue

Zwetschge (Austrian, *Zwetschke*) plum; *Zwetschgendatschi* (South German), plum cake; *Zwetschgenknödel* (South German), plum dumpling

Zwiebel onion; *Wiener Zwiebelsauce* (Austrian), onion and garlic sauce; *Zwiebelfleisch* (Austrian), onion and beef casserold; *Zwiebelkuchen* (Austrian), savoury flan with onions, tomatoes and bacon; *Zwiebeltorte*, savoury flan with onions; *Zwiebelsuppe*, onion soup

Italy

Land of *pasta* and *pizza*, *risotto* and *ragù*, Italy has so many seemingly familiar dishes, cheerfully taken over and reproduced by expatriate Italians and non-Italians alike far from their native soil. Yet nothing can compare with eating Italian food in Italy, where no region can ever adopt a dish without providing its own distinctive hallmark – a herb typical of that region, a splash of the local wine, or a sprinkling of home-produced cheese. Even when you think you know exactly what to expect of a particular dish, a new locality will produce a fresh version.

Pasta is of course the regional food *par excellence*: every region has its own speciality, and sometimes its own name for a common type (for example, the Emilians call ribbon noodles *fettucine*, which are known elsewhere as *tagliatelle*). If you like *pasta*, you will be pretty safe with anything that appears under that heading on the restaurant menu, because a long, unfamiliar name is likely to denote a fanciful, locally-devised shape rather than the inclusion of any unfamiliar ingredients.

Pasta is certainly Italy's favourite food, and many Italians eat it twice a day without a thought to their waistlines: what is more, they regard it as a mere prelude to the main course of the meal. Even Christmas lunch is incomplete without pasta, as far as many Italians are concerned. And of course it is always better for being *fatta in casa* – home-made; there is simply no comparison between the rather dried-out, tired-tasting stuff we usually buy from the supermarkets and the freshly made version, wherever you happen to be eating it.

The real home of the *pizza* is Naples, but you will find it throughout the country, and indeed, if you do not want to indulge in a full-scale meal it makes the ideal lunchtime standby. Failing *pizza*, do not forget the wonderful country cheeses and delicatessen-type sausages, including the well-known *mortadella* and *salami*, which can sometimes be easier to track down than a restaurant that serves snacks.

European Menu Guide

But Italy is so much more than *pizza* and *pasta*. As with France, Italy's great strength lies in the range of its provincial cooking; from the spring lamb of Rome to the hearty mountain food of Umbria, fish from the Adriatic, pork from Emilia-Romagna, *risotto* from Milan, olives and figs from Calabria. This wealth of variety will provide the traveller with a constant source of pleasure.

Virtually all Italian restaurants are informal and usually very friendly – and if you have children, you need never worry that they will not be welcomed.

Buon appetito!

Phrases For The Restaurant

I want to reserve a table for.... at....
Vorrei riservare un tavolo per .... alle....
Have you a table for......
Avete un tavolo per......
A quiet table
Un posto tranquillo
A table near the window
Un tavolo vicino alla finestra
A table on the terrace
U tavolo sulla terrazza
Could we have another table please?
Potremmo avere un altro tavolo, per favore?
I am in a hurry/we are in a hurry
Sono di fretta/Siamo di fretta
Please bring me the menu
Può darmi il menu, per favore
Can we have ...... please
Possiamo avere un ...... per favore
Local dishes
Piatti locali
How much is it?
Quanto costa?
What is it?
Che cos'è?
I did not order this
Non ho ordinato questo
Too much
Troppo, grazie
More
Ancòra, per favore
The bill please
Il conto per favore
Is service included?
È compreso il servizo?
I think there is a mistake in the bill
Penso che ci sia un errore nel conto
Do you accept travellers' cheques?
Accettate i traveller's cheques?

Restaurant Terms

antipasto
('before the meal'), starter, hors d'oeuvre

bicchiere
glass

buongustai
gourmets

caldo
hot

cameriere
waiter

conto
bill

coperto
cover (charge)

cena
supper

colazione
lunch

dente, al
literally 'to the tooth', i.e. not over-cooked but still with a firm texture; a term used to describe the ideal point to which pasta, rice and certain vegetables should be cooked

dolci
sweets, cakes and pastries

freddo
cold

fresco
fresh, cool

giorno, del
(dish) of the day

menu
menu

minestra, minestre
first course, or soup course; soups

pasto
meal

piatti
dishes; da farsi, cooked to order; de giorno, of the day

pizzeria
 pizza restaurant
pranzo
 dinner
prezzo fisso
 fixed price
ristorante
 restaurant
tavola
 table; calda, 'hot table', restaurant primarily for quick lunches, taken standing or sitting
trattoria
 restaurant

Menu Terms

abbacchio Roman dialect word for baby lamb, an Easter speciality of the region; often spit-roasted or cooked in the oven (*al forno*) with rosemary; *alla cacciatora* (hunter's-style), braised with olive oil, vinegar, sage, rosemary and garlic, and served with a sauce also including anchovies (celebrated Roman speciality); *brodettato*, cut into pieces with a sauce of olive oil, white wine, garlic, egg and lemon; *alla scottadito*, cutlets, grilled

acciuga, acciughe anchovy, anchovies (see *alici*), common garnish for pizza; *carne ai capperi e*, veal with a sauce of capers, anchovies and herbs (Umbrian dish)

aceto vinegar

affumicato smoked

agliata, all' in garlic sauce

aglio garlic

agnello lamb; *all'arrabbiata* ('angry'), cooked over a very high flame and sprinkled with salt, pepper and vinegar; *bistecchine fritte di*, fried chops; *e fagioli alla toscana*, Tuscan casserole of lamb and beans, with garlic and herbs; *in fricassea*, fricassee; *con sottaceti*, cooked with olive oil, white wine, rosemary, garlic and pickled vegetables; *trippato*, in egg sauce; *alla veneziana* (Venetian-style), cooked in milk; see also *abbacchio*

agnolotti type of pasta, cresent-shaped, served with various stuffings; *alla piemontese* (Piedmont-style), stuffed with minced veal and ham, cheese, egg and nutmeg

agoni variety of shad, usually cooked in sage-flavoured butter

agrodolce sweet-sour sauce, made of honey, sugar, vinegar and lemon juice

aguglie garfish, green-boned species served either fried or stewed in a sauce of tomatoes, onions and oregano

albicocche apricots

alici anchovies; *al gratin*, fresh, oven-baked with breadcrumb topping; *all'ischiana* (Ischia-style), fresh, oven-baked with olive oil, lemon juice and wild marjoram

alla, al, all' in the style of, or simply 'with'

allodole larks

alloro bay

amaretti miniature macaroons, often served with the coffee after a meal

amatriciana see *bucatini*

ananas pineapple

anara regional name for duck in the Veneto

anguilla eel; *arrosta*, roast; *al girarrosto*, cooked on a spit; *risotto adriatico all'*, risotto with eels from the Adriatic (speciality of Ravenna); *in umido al vino*, stewed with wine, tomato purée and bay leaves; *alla valligiana* (in the style of the valley), split open and cooked in its own juices, sprinkled with pepper

animelle sweetbreads

anitra duck; *ripiena*, roast, and stuffed with its own liver, veal, bacon, Parmesan, breadcrumbs, egg and herbs; *alla salsa piccante*, in a piquant sauce; *alla valligiana* (in the syle of the valley), stuffed with its own offal, bacon, herbs and onion and boiled

anolini type of pasta, usually served stuffed with spinach or with *stracotto*

antipasto ('before the meal'), starter, appetizer, *hors d'oeuvre*

anzio pie see *pasticcio di maccheroni all'anziana*

aragosta rock lobster, langouste or crayfish (not the true lobster, but the type most commonly found in the Mediterranean); *frittelle di*, lobster fritters, pieces fried in batter and served with mayonnaise

arancia, aranci orange(s); *al caramel* (or *arranci caramellizzati*), sliced and served in caramelized juice; *ripiene*, filled with other fruit; *tagliati*, macerated slices of

arancine balls of fried rice with chopped meat and *caciocavallo* cheese

arigusta rock lobster, langouste or crayfish (see *aragosta*)

aringhe herrings

àrista loin of pork; *alla fiorentina* (Florence-style), slow-roasted with rosemary, garlic and clove; *di maiale arrosto*, roast; *perugina* (Perugia-style), roast pork with fennel

arrabbiata 'angry', usually denoting the use of strong flavourings or sometimes simply that the dish is cooked over a high flame

European Menu Guide

arrosto roast

arrosito grilled

arrotolato stuffed

arselle clams (Genoese and Sardinian name)

ascuitta dry (especially of pasta and pasta dishes)

asiago sharp, granular mountain cheese made from partly skimmed cow's milk in the Veneto region

asparagi asparagus; *alla fiorentina* (Florence-style), boiled, tossed in butter with Parmesan and seasoning, and topped with fried eggs; *punti di*, tips of

baccalà dried, salted cod, also known as *stoccafisso*, stockfish; *alla fiorentina* (Florence-style), with oil, garlic and pepper; *mantecata* ('worked'), creamed, with milk, oil and garlic; *alla veneziana* (Venetian-style), cooked with butter, milk and flour, onions and anchovy; *alla vicentina*, variant of the latter, from Vicenza

bagna cauda hot cocktail dip or sauce made of anchovy and garlic

balsamella béchamel (see *besciamella*)

banana banana

barbabietola beetroot

barbuta brill

beccaccino snipe

basilico basil

bel paese ('beautiful country'), mild, creamy cheese made in Lombardy

ben cotta well cooked (of steak)

besciamella béchamel sauce, basic mixture of flour, butter and milk which is essential to many pasta dishes, including *lasagne*

bianchetta whitebait

bianco white; used of sauces, in particular, to denote the absence of tomatoes; *in bianco*, boiled

biete Swiss chard

bignè deep-fried pastry puffs

bigoli type of pasta, Venetian name for a sort of *cannelloni*; *coi rovinazzi*, cockscombs and sage

birra beer

bisati eels

bistecca beef or veal steak; *alla pizzaiola*, with tomato and garlic sauce; *alla fiorentina* (Florence-style), porter-house, grilled over charcoal; see also *al sangue*, *a puntino* and *ben cotta*

bitto country cheese from Lombardy made from a mixture of cow's and goat's milk

bocconcini 'mouth pleasers', see *olivette*

bollito boiled (meat); *misto*, classic dish of various boiled meats and haricot beans, from Piedmont

bolognese generally denoting a (meat-) gravy and tomato sauce

bombette little 'bombs', or balls

bomboline del ricotta in brodo soup with dumplings made of ricotta cheese

bombolini doughnuts

bonnarelli Roman name for thin ribbon pasta also known as *tagliolini*

bonito a small tunny fish

bòsega clams

bottarga tuna eggs either toasted or seasoned with oil and lemon

bovolo sea-snail

brace, alla on the embers, grilled

braciole thin slices of meat, usually rolled round a filling

braciolette slices of veal wrapped round ham or other filling

bracioline cutlets

branzino sea bass

brasato braised; *alls bresciana* (Brescia-style), beef braised in oil and red wine, with onions, garlic and bacon; *di manzo*, braised beef

bresaola dried salt beef, served thinly sliced as a starter with oil and lemon juice

broccoli broccoli; *alla romana* (Roman-style), sautéed with garlic in white wine and olive oil; *alla siciliana* (Sicilian-style), cooked with red wine, olive oil, onion, olives, anchovies and Parmesan cheese

brodetto ('little broth'), rather liquid fish stew, or soup, from Ravenna, containing squid, red mullet, sea bass, eel and shellfish, tomatoes, herbs, usually some saffron, and garlic; possibly with slices of bread floating in it

European Menu Guide

brodo (ristretto) clear soup or broth; *di cappone*, chicken consommé; *di manzo*, beef stock; *pasta in*, *con fegatini e fagioli/lenticchie/piselli*, pasta in chicken stock with chicken livers and haricot beans/lentils/peas

bucatini type of pasta (also called *perciatelli*) resembling thick, hollow spaghetti; *all'amatriciana*, served with a sauce of tomatoes, bacon, chillis and pecorino cheese

buccallato ring-shaped fruitcake, its centre filled with wine-marinated strawberries

budino pudding, dessert; *di prugne*, flan filled with prunes and other dried fruits, nuts, lemon peel, Marsala and cream; *toscano* (Tuscan), baked cheese mold with amonds and dried fruit

bue beef

burrida Genoese name for *brodetto*

burrini same as *buttiri*

burro butter; *salsa di*, butter sauce made with wine, parsley and onion

busecca highly seasoned veal tripe, served with beans (speciality of Lombardy region)

buttiri a Calabrian version of the cheese *cacio a cavallo* which has fresh butter in its centre

cacciagione game, venison

cacciatora, alla hunter's-style, usually describing poultry, fish or game cooked in a simple sauce: e.g. braised with olive oil, white wine, herbs and vegetables (mushrooms, tomatoes, spring onions)

cacciucco (livornese) fish stew (speciality of Leghorn, Livorno) containing octopus, squid, lobster and crab, white wine, tomato sauce and garlic (not unlike the *bouillabaisse* of southern France)

cacio a cavallo, caciocavallo cheese of similar type to *provolone*

caciotta romana semi-hard, sweet sheep's-milk cheese rom Rome and its environs (Lazio or Latium region)

caciotto general name for local cheese which is made from either cow's or sheep's milk in the Marches, from goat's milk in Capri, and from sheep's milk in Tuscany and Umbria

caffè (*espresso*) coffee, black, strong and aromatic, served in a small cup; see also *cappucino*

caffelatte coffee and hot milk in equal proportions

calamaretti baby squid; *del Golfo fritte*, from the Bay of Biscay, deep fried

calamari squid; *fritti*, fried; *e piselli alla livornese*, Livorno-style, with peas; *in umido*, stewed in red wine

calzoni (1) small egg pasta envelopes, like ravioli, usually filled with meat: (2) Neopolitan version of pizza with the crust folded round the base like a turnover

canestrato Sicilian sheep's milk cheese

cannarozzetti type of pasta, name used in the Abruzzi for *ditalini* or *tubetti* (short, ribbed pasta)

cannella cinnamon

cannellini dried haricot or kidney beans, served with an oil-and-vinegar dressing

cannelloni type of pasta, large tubes of noodle dough filled with a meat and béchamel mixture and baked

cannoli tubes of crisp pastry stuffed with ricotta cheese, candied fruit and chocolate, a Sicilian speciality

capelli d'angelo 'angel hair', type of pasta; very fine noodles usually served in a meat broth with Parmesan cheese sprinkled over

capitone large eel

capòn capon; *alla canevera*, sewn into a pig's bladder with pieces of guinea-fowl and beef

caponata, caponatina (di melanzane or alla siciliana) Sicilian dish of cooked vegetables, based on sautéed aubergines and including tomatoes, celery, capers and olives, possible with anchovy or anchovy juice (Catanian version); in Palermo seafood ingredients are added

capporozzoli clams

cappe clams

cappellacci type of pasta usually served stuffed with pumpkin (see *zucca*) and peculiar to Ferrara

cappelletti 'little hats', type of pasta; dumplings stuffed with chicken, pork, *mortadella*, ricotta, Parmesan and nutmeg; *alla bolognese*, with gravy and tomato sauce

capperi capers

cappuccino coffee made with hot, foaming milk, and sometimes served sprinkled with finely grated chocolate

European Menu Guide

capretto kid, young goat; *alla cacciatora* (hunter's style), cooked with onion and white wine; *ripieno al forno*, stuffed with herbs and roasted; *al vino bianco*, braised in white wine and Marsala, with herbs and vegetables

capriata purée of dried beans and olive oil served with green vegetables or pimentos, onion and tomato

capriolo roe-deer; *in umido*, venison stew; *alla valdostana* (Val d'Aosta-style), cooked in white wine and brandy, with white truffles and cheese

carciofi globe artichokes; *alla crema*, in a cream sauce; *alla giudia* (Jewish-style), young whole artichokes, deep fried, usually with parsley and garlic (Roman speciality); *di insalata*, sliced with lemon juice and oil; *alla manticiana*, grilled; *ripieni*, filled with anchovies, garlic and breadcrumbs and braised in wine; *alla romana* (Roman-style), young whole artichokes casseroled with meat and garlic; *alla veneziana* (Venetian style), braised in oil and white wine

cardi chards; *alla bagna cauda*, Piedmontese dish with a hot sauce including shredded garlic, anchovies, cream and truffles

carne meat; sometimes denotes veal (see *acciughe*)

carote carrots

carpione carp

carrozza, in 'in a carriage': Neapolitan term applying especially to fried mozzarella cheese sandwiches

carte di giuoco ('card-game'), type of pasta, irregularly shaped served with tomato and sometimes mutton and also known as *stracci*

cartoccio oiled paper case, or tinfoil, in which food is cooked

casalinga, (alla) homemade, home-style

casereccio homemade

cassata ice-cream dish in which a shell of cream or chocolate encases lighter ice-cream; *(alla) siciliana*, Sicilian sponge-cake frosted with chocolate and containing ricotta, mixed candied fruit and, frequently, ice-cream

castagne chestnuts; *al marsala*, cooked in marsala and red wine with sugar and served either hot or cold with cream

cavolfiori cauliflower; *saltati al burro e aglio*, sautéed in butter with garlic

cavoli-cappucci brussels sprouts; *agrodolci*, with sweet and sour sauce

cavolini di Bruxelles Brussels sprouts

cavolirape kohl rabi

cavolo cabbage

cazzuola stew; *di montone alla fiorentina*, of mutton, Florence-style, with pig-meat, beans or pasta, tomato sauce and vegetables, with a fried-breadcrumb topping

ceci chick peas; *e castagne*, with roasted chestnuts; *di Navelli*, on fried bread with a sauce of olive oil, onion and rosemary

cedro citron

cee baby eels; *alla viagreggina* (Viareggio-style), with tomatoes, garlic, herbs and wine

cefalo grey mullet, usually served roasted or grilled

cenci alla fiorentina crisp-fried sweet pastries

cervella, cervelli (calves') brains; *al burro nero*, in black butter; *dorate alla milanese* (Milan-style), in egg and breadcrumbs, fried

cervellada sausage made from pork fat, cheese, marrow, and spices

cervo venison; *con salsa di ciliegie*, with cherry sauce

cetroli cucumbers

chiodi di girofano cloves

cicoria chicory

cieche elvers (young eels), served in Pisa cooked in oil with sage

ciliegii cherries

cima breast (of animal); also, particularly, cold stuffed veal (*di vitello*), a popular dish of Genoa, sometimes so described (*alla genovese*), the stuffing consisting of veal offal and leg meat, eggs, artichokes, Parmesan cheese and peas; it can be bought by weight in *rosticcerie* (cooked-food shops)

cinghiale wild boar; *in agrodolce*, with sweet-sour sauce; *arrosto*, roast; *alla cacciatora*, (hunter's-style), braised in white wine and stock with vegetables; *stufato di*, stew

cioccolato chocolate; *budino*, or *spuma di*, mousse

cipolle onions

cipolline chives, shallots, spring onions; *in agrodolce*, tiny spring onions in thin sweet-sour tomato sauce

European Menu Guide

cocciule clams (Sardinia)

cocomero watermelon

coda tail; *di bue alla vaccinara*, oxtail, butcher's-style (Roman speciality, braised with wine and vegetables)

conchiglia small shellfish

conchiglie type of pasta resembling sea-shells

condito seasoned, tasty

coniglio rabbit; *bollito al sale aromatico*, stewed with herbs, lemon and garlic; *fritto dorato*, marinated, coated in egg and flour and fried; *alla livornese* (Livorno-style), sautéed in tomato sauce with garlic, onion and anchovy; *alla portoghese* (Portuguese style), stewed with vegetables

consomme all'uova beef consommé poured over mixture of lemon juice and beated eggs, sprinkled with grated cheese

contorni vegetables served to accompany or garnish a main course

coppa (1) in Rome, brawn made from pig's head: (2) in the Veneto, a meat loaf made with layers of ham, tongue and *mortadella*

coratella offal, e.g. hearts, lungs, liver, kidney

coscetto leg (often, of lamb)

coscia leg

cosciotti, cosciotto legs, leg; *di rane fritte*, deep-fried frog's legs

costa rib, chop

costata fillet steak or rib chop; *alla fiorentina* (Florence-style), grilled fillet of veal cooked with oil and seasoning; *alla pizzaiola*, with tomatoes, garlic and wild marjoram (Campania)

costolette cutlets, chops (same as cotolette); *di agnello alla marinetti*, lamb, braised in white wine with herbs; *alla bolognese* (Bologna-style), veal cutlet, coated in egg, topped with a slice of ham and melted cheese; *di maiale*, pork chops; *(di vitello) alla milanese*, breaded veal cutlet (a rib chop), Milan-style, cooked in butter and garnished with lemon and parsley; *di vitello alla valdostana* (Val d'Aosta-style), sautéed veal, stuffed with *fontina* cheese

costolettine small chops; *di agnello fritte*, lamb rib chops fried in Parmesan cheese batter

cotechino highly spiced sausage made from pork (Roman speciality); *con fagioli*, boiled, with (haricot) beans; *con lenticchie*, with lentils (New Year Dish)

cotolettine see *costolettine*

cotto cooked, done; *a puntino*, just to the right amount (of steak, medium rare)

cozze mussels; *alla marinara* (sailor-style), marinated in white wine and oil; *al vino bianco*, cooked in white wine with garlic and parsley and served cold

crema custard or cream; *caramella*, crème caramel; *di piselli* (*di pollo*, *di pomodoro*) cream of pea (chicken, tomato) soup

crescione watercress

crespelle pancakes; served in Lombardy wrapped round chopped meat and served with a cheese sauce

crespolini thin pancakes, served filled with Parmesan and cream cheese, spinach and chicken livers, with a topping of Parmesan and mozzarella cheese and béchamel sauce

crocchette croquettes; *di cervella*, made with calf's brain, pounded into a paste, dipped into egg and flour and fried in butter

crostacei shellfish

crosta (di torta), crostata, crostatina (pie-) crust, tart; *crostata alla napoletana* (Naples-style), chocolate cream pie with apricots; *di ricotta*, cheesecake; *alla siciliana* (Sicilian-style), open pie containing creamy filling with orange and lemon peel and chopped pistachio nuts

crostini croûtons, or small cubes of fried bread, often spread with cheese; *di fegatini*, with chopped chicken livers and ham; *alla provatura*, dipped in egg and baked with a piece of buffalo-milk cheese (*provatura* or *mozzarella*) on top

crudo raw

cupete soft pastries made with honey, sugar and walnuts

cuscusu couscous, speciality of Sicily

datteri dates; *di mare*, shellfish, or 'sea dates', particular kind of delicate-flavoured Mediterranean shellfish found off Genoese coast and used in soups

dentice dentex, type of fish found in Mediterranean waters, usually served grilled or roasted

diavola, alla devilled, often denoting the inclusion of chillis or other hot flavours in the sauce

disossato boned

dolce sardo soft cheese from Sardinia

dolci desserts, sweets, cakes; *dolce mafarka*, rice mould flavoured with coffee, lemon and orange-flower water

dorato gilded, golden brown

dragoncello tarragon

endivia see *indivia*

erbe herbs

erbette greens

escaloppe escalopes; *alla milanese*, fried veal, with parsley and lemon

escarole Batavian endive

espresso see *caffè*

fagiano pheasant; *arrosto*, roast; *con funghi e besciamella*, with mushrooms and béchamel sauce; *con crema e tartufi*, with cream and truffles

fagioli dried kidney beans or haricots; *alla fiorentina* (Florence-style), with oil, herbs and onions; *minestrone di*, in soup with celery and tomatoes, Tuscan speciality; *in salsa*, salad of boiled beans eaten cold with anchovies and an oil-and-vinegar dressing

fagiolini French, or string, beans; *col tonno*, with tuna fish

fagottini bundles; *di vitello leccabaffi*, veal, with anchovies and cheese

farcito stuffed

farfalle ('butterflies'), type of pasta, so-called because of their shape, sometimes served with a sauce of *prosciutto* and tomato

farfalline ('little butterflies'), type of pasta, containing egg, in the shape of a butterfly

farina flour

farinacei farinaceous (cereal) dishes

fave broad beans

fegato liver; *alla veneziana* (Venetian style), calf's, with onions

fegatelli liver; *di maiale alla toscana*, pork (Tuscan-style), either spit-roasted or fried with breadcrumbs, Parmesan and herbs with olive oil and red wine

fegatini (de pollo) chicken livers

feraona guinea-fowl

ferri, ai ('on the irons'), grilled

fetta, fettina slice, little (or thin) slice

fettucine egg noodles, type of pasta; name used in Emilia region for *tagliatelle* (ribbon noodles or strip macaroni); *al burro*, with butter (Roman speciality); *al doppio burro*, or *all'Alfredo*, tossed in butter, cream and Parmesan cheese; *alla marinara* (sailor-style), Neapolitan dish with fresh tomato sauce and basil; *all'uovo*, buttered egg noodles

fichi figs; celebratd in Sicily, commonly included in fruit salads and sometimes eaten with Parma ham; *d'India* ('Indian figs'), prickly pears, eaten throughout southern Italy

filetto fillet

finanziera di pollo chicken livers, mushrooms, sweetbreads and truffles in a meat and tomato sauce, presented in a pastry shell (Piedmontese speciality)

finocchi fennel; *al burro e fromaggio*, sautéed, with butter and Parmesan; *fritti*, fried; *all'olio*, braised in olive oil

fiorentina, alla Florence-style, often alluding to the inclusion of spinach

fiorentina, la grilled steak, Florence-style: T-bone steak flavoured with crushed peppercorns

focaccia Genoese name for pizza

foiolo tripe

fondi (di carciofo) (artichoke) hearts

fonduta Piedmontese dish of melted (*fontina*) cheese with milk, eggs and sometimes grated white truffles, a speciality of Piedmont; *alla parmigiana*, made from alternative layers of sliced Parmesan, white truffles and grated Parmesan, melted in the oven

fontina Piedmontese cheese, like a fat, creamy gruyère, used in *fonduta*; true *fontina* comes from the Val d'Aosta region

formaggio cheese; *di grana*, Parmesan

forno, al in the oven, oven-baked

fragole, fragoline stawberries; *di bosco*, *dei boschi*, wood (wild); *di mare*, sea strawberries or baby squid (same as *moscardini* and *polpetti*)

freddo cold

fresco uncooked, raw

European Menu Guide

fricassea fricassee

frittata omelette; *affogata* ('drowned'), omelette steeped in tomato sauce, a Tuscan speciality; *al fromaggion*, cheese; *genovese*, Genoese, with spinach

frittatina small omelette or pancake; *di cipolle*, onion omelette; *imbottita*, stuffed pancakes, with a filling (e.g. of cheese or cheese and spinach)

frittelle pastry puffs or fritters, filled with cheese, shellfish or other items and served deep-fried and very hot; *di San Giuseppe* (speciality for St Joseph's Day), rice fritters made with lemon and orange peel and marsala

fritto, fritte fried (e.g. potatoes, *patate fritte*)

fritto misto mixed fry or grill; *di mare*, fish

frittura mista mixed fry or grill (Milanese name for *fritto misto*)

frutta fruit; *candita*, candied, speciality of Sicily; *cotta*, stewed; *insalata di*, salad; *di mare*, seafood, assorted shellfish; *di stagione*, of the season

funghi mushrooms; *fritti*, fried, in batter; *alla genovese* (Genoa-style), sprinkled with pepper, cooked in olive oil on grape leaves and eaten with cloves; *alla graticola*, grilled; *ripieni*, stuffed, with Parmesan, bacon or ham, garlic, herbs and optionally, breadcrumbs; *stufati* ('smothered'), in tomatoes, garlic and hers; *trifolati*, sautéed, with garlic and parsley; *in umido*, stewed, in olive oil with garlic and mint

galantina boned meat, game, poultry or fish, stuffed and served cold

gallina hen

gamberi shrimps, large prawns; *dorati*, fried in batter; *di fiume* (river), crayfish

gamberetti prawns

gambero di mare true lobster, rarely found in Mediterranean waters (see *aragosta*)

gamberoni large sea prawns of the Genoese coast

garganelli (From a verb meaning 'to gulp down'), type of homemade egg pasta, quill-shaped with ridged surface, speciality of Romagna served with *ragu* or a sauce of cream and *prosciutto*

gasse type of pasta in the shape of bows, served with *pesto* or in broth on the Italian Riviera

gelato ice-cream; *di albicocche*, apricot; *di banana al rum*, flavoured with banana and rum; *di caffe*, coffee; *di cioccolata*, chocolate; *di fragole*, strawberry; *di nocciol*a, hazelnut; *di torrone*, nougat

genovese, alla Genoa-style, sometimes denoting the presence of fish

ghiaccio, ghiacciato ice, iced

gioddù Sardinian yoghurt

girarrosto, al spit-roasted

girato (al fuoco di legna) spit-roasted (over wood fire); *misto*, mixed spit-roast, with different meats such as poultry, pork and sausage

gnocchetti miniature dumplings, type of pasta; *cacio e ova*, cheese and egg, also containig pieces of bacon (known colloquially as *strangolapreti*)

gnocchi small dumplings, type of pasta; *del casentino*, made with spinach and ricotta; *di parmigiana*, made with Parmesan and served as an appetizer; *di patate*, made from potatoes and flour; *col pesto*, with pesto sauce; *alla piemontese*, (Piedmont-style), served with a brown sauce and Parmesan cheese; *di polenta*, made of yellow maize flour; *di ricotta*, made from ricotta cheese and flour; *alla romana* (Roman-style), semolina dumplings, cooked in tomato sauce, topped wih cheese and placed under the grill; *verdi*, made from spinach and ricotta cheese (northern Italian speciality)

gorgonzola strong, mellow, blue-veined cow's-milk cheese from Lombardy region

gramigna type of egg pasta, short and curled, served with a sauce containing cream and sausage (speciality of the Emilia-Romagna region)

grana (1) grain: (2) hard, coarse-textured cheese (particularly Parmesan)

granceole, grancevole large Adriatic spider-crabs, bright red in colour

granchio crab

granite flavoured water-ices with the texture of shaved ice, not usually served as a dessert but eaten as a refreshment in cafés; *al caffè*, coffee; *di fragole*, strawberry; *di limone*, lemon; *con panna*, with whipped cream

granotuco sweetcorn

granseole veneziane Venetian dish of local variety of crab

grappa brandy made by fermented grape skins and pips that remain after juice has been drawn off

gremolata, gremolada mixture of chopped parsley, garlic and lemon peel traditionally served with *osso bucco*

griglia, alla grilled

grissini bread sticks (originally from Turin)

groviera Italian gruyère

gropetti slices of veal wrapped round ham or other stuffing

imbottito stuffed

impanato breaded

indivia endive

insalata salad; *di frutta*, fruit; *verde*, green; *mista*, mixed; *di pomodoro*, tomato

involtini slices of veal wrapped round ham or other stuffing

lampone raspberries

lardo salt pork; *affumicato*, bacon

lasagne type of pasta, thin slices of pasta cooked in the oven (*al forno*) with a béchamel sauce, a meat and tomato sauce, and cheese; *alla piemontese*, with the addition of white truffles; *verde*, same pasta made with spinach, cooked in a similar fashion

latte milk; *maiale al*, pork cooked in milk; *patate al*, potatoes cooked in milk, but not mashed; *pollo al*, cooked in milk

lattemiele whipped cream, speciality of Milan

latticini fresh mountain cheeses

lattuga lettuce; *ripiena* ('stuffed'), cooked in beef consommé and served with gravy, Easter speciality of La Spezia

lattume soft tuna roe

lauro bay (leaf, leaves)

legumi vegetables

lenticchie lentils; *in umido*, stewed, with onion, garlic, mint and olive oil

lepre hare; *in agrodolce*, in sweet-sour sauce; *arrosto di*, *con senape e brandy*, roast, with mustard and brandy; *alla cacciatora* (hunter's-style), cooked in a sauce of oil, sage, garlic and rosemary; *alla montana*, or *alla montnura*, mountain-style, casseroled with red wine, pine kernels, sultanas, sugar and cinnamon; *in salami*, pot-roasted and served in a sauce containing wine and its own liver; *in umido*, stewed; *alla veneta*, cooked on the spit (Paduan speciality)

lesso, lesse boiled (e.g. potatoes, *patate lesse*)

limone lemon

lingua tongue; *di bue*, ox; *in salsa*, served in a sauce of white wine, chopped anchovy and capers

linguine type of pasta, like thin, flat spaghetti, usually eaten with meat sauce; *alla romana* (Roman-style), cooked in butter with ricotta cheese

livornese, alla Livorno-style, usually with fish, garlic, tomato and parsley

lonza cured fillet of pork, flavoured with wine, spices and garlic, cut in thin slices and served raw as a starter

luganega, luganica a long, curling, sweet sausage

lumache snails; *in zimino*, stewed in oil with onion, garlic, mushrooms and herbs

maccaroncelli type of pasta, like thick, tubular spaghetti

maccheroni macaroni, type of pasta, in thick tubes; *alla chitarra*, cut into strips on the wires of a guitar- (*chitarra*-) shaped utensil (speciality of Abruzzi region); *al forno*, cooked in the oven with tomatoes, mushrooms, cheese and a white sauce; *con gamberi*, with shrimps (Pescaran speciality); *alla marinara* (sailor style), with tomato sauce; *alla napolentana* (Naples-style), with tomatoes and basil; *pasticcio di, all'anziana*, Anzion macaroni pie (see *pasticcio*); *alle vongole*, with a clam and tomato sauce

macedonia di frutta fruit salad

maggiorana marjoram

magro lean

maiale pork; *arrosto di, all'alloro*, roast, with bay leaves; *arrosto di, al latte*, cooked in milk; *bistecche di*, chops; *costa di, alla griglia*, marinated pork chops, cooked under the grill; *fegatelli di, alla toscana*, liver, Tuscan-style, either spit-roasted or fried with breadcrumbs, parmesan and herbs with olive oil and red wine; *ubriaco* ('drunken'), in red wine

maionese mayonnaise (made only with oil, eggs and lemon juice)

European Menu Guide

maltagliati ('badly cut'), type of short pasta used for soups, especially soups that include beans or chick peas

mandorie almonds

manicotti type of pasta, large tubes served stuffed and baked with a sauce

mantecato worked, creamed

manzo beef; *bollito*, boiled; *alla bresciana* (Brescia-style), casseroled with salt pork, garlic, butter and red wine; *brodo di*, consommé; *costa di*, *al vino rosso*, rib of, marinated in red wine; *fettine di*, *alla sorrentina*, thin steaks Sorrento-style, with tomatoes and olives; *alla lonbarda* (Lombardy-style), braised, then cooked with parsley, carrots, onion and celery in red wine; *ripieno arrosto*, stuffed roast; *stufato di*, *alla genovese*, Genoese beef stew

marasca morello cherry

maraschino liqueur brandy made from cherries

mare, al sea-style, denoting the inclusion of seafood

marinara, alla sailor-style; southern Italian sauce with tomato, oregano, oil and garlic

marinato marinated

maritozzi (romani) small soft buns made with egg dough and raisins (Lenten speciality in Rome area)

marsala dark, strong, amber-coloured and semi-sweet Sicilian wine, not unlike a heavy sherry

masanète clams

mascarpone, mascherpone small fresh double-cream cheeses marketed in individual muslin-wrapped cylinders; *crema di*, served with fruit or sugar, or sugar and maraschino, or with powdered chocolate; alternatively, sometimes eaten with liqueurs

mazzacuogni, mazzancolle very large prawns, like scampi

mela apple

melanzane aubergines; *funghetti*, sautéed in small pieces, with skin left on; *alla parmigiana*, baked with Parmesan and mozzarella cheese; *ripiene*, stuffed, with anchovy fillets, olives, garlic, capers, parsley and bread

melone melon

menta mint

merluzzo cod

messicaini (di vitello) con risotto ('Mexicans with risotto'), rolls of veal stuffed with meat, cheese, bread, garlic, spices and egg, cooked in wine or spit-roasted and basted with wine

miele honey

migliaccio cake made of chestnut flour to accompany *uccelletti*, small birds

mille foglie ('Thousand leaves', cf. French *mille feuilles*), flaky pastry

minestra, minestre soup or pasta course; thick vegetable soup; *torinese*, vegetable soup with saffron and garlic

minestrone thick vegetable soup (literally 'big soup'), sometimes including rice and usually sprinkled with Parmesan cheese; *alla genovese*, with pesto; *alla milanese*, with green vegetables, rice and bacon

misto mixed

mitili mussels

monte bianco 'white mountain', dessert made with puréed chestnut and chocolate, rum, sugar and cream

montone mutton

morbido soft, tender

morene lampreys or sea-eels

mortadella large, spiced pork sausage, speciality of Bologna

moscardini sea strawberries or baby squid (same as *fragoline di mare* and *polpetti*)

mostarda mustard (usually French); also candied fruits in mustard syrup, a sort of chutney, made in Cremona

mozzarella soft white buffalo-milk cheese, a Neapolitan speciality and one of the staple ingredients for *pizza* toppings; also served fried and baked; *in carrozza* ('in a carriage'), cheese savoury, fried cheese sandwich

muscoli mussels

Napoli, napolitana Naples, Neapolitan, with tomatoes and basil

nocchette type of pasta made with egg (same as *farfalline*)

nocciola hazelnut; *gelato di*, ice-cream

noce nut, walnut; *di cocco*, coconut; *salsa di*, sauce, made with walnuts, oil, parsley and cream; *moscata*, nutmeg

oca goose; *di Treviso*, cooked with celery

olio oil; *di oliva*, olive

European Menu Guide

olivia olive

olivette slices of veal wrapped round ham, Parmesan and parsley

ombrina Mediterranean fish (L. *Ombrina leccia*) with firm white flesh, similar to sea bass and usually served boiled (*in bianco*)

orata large Mediterranean fish with silver scales, usually cooked with liquid (*al vino bianco*, for example)

orecchiette ('little ears'), type of pasta, small discs of pasta pushed into an ear-shape with the thumb; speciality of Apulia often served with a sauce containing broccoli and anchovies

origano oregano

ortaggi vegetable dishes

osso buco ('bone with a hole in it'), shin, or knuckle, of veal, cooked in wine and stock with tomatoes and served with rice; *alla milanese*, Milan-style (the dish originated in Milan)

ostriche oysters (Taranto is famous for them); *alla veneziana* (Venice-style), with caviar

paesana, la dessert of white raisins soaked in eau-de-vie (spirit, often fruit flavoured)

paesana, alla peasant- or country-style; sauce made with bacon, Parmesan cheese and mushrooms

paeta regional name for turkey in the Veneto

pagello sea bream

paglia e fieno ('straw and hay'), yellow and green pasta served with a cream sauce (*alla ghiotta*, glutton-style)

palombacci game pigeons

pancetta bacon

pane bread

panettone large fruit cake, or spiced brioche, from Lombardy region, containing candied lemon peel and raisins or sultanas; a popular Christmas present

panforte sugar cake made with honey, almonds, and candied melon, orange or lemon (speciality of Siena)

panini bread rolls

panna cream; *montata*, whipped; *alla parmigiana*, with Parmesan cheese

pannerone a white version of gorgonzola, sometimes called

gorgonzola bianco

pappa al pomodoro, la Florentine soup made with bread, tomatoes and fresh basil

pappardelle type of pasta, very broad noodles with crimped edges; *all'arrabbiata* ('angry'), with a sauce of tomatoes, chillis and bacon; *con la lepre*, Tuscan speciality, with a sauce of wild hare, wine and cheese

parmigiana, alla sprinkled with Parmesan cheese (sometimes also denoting the presence of Parma ham); alternatively, may denote a dish from Parma

parmigiano Parmesan cheese (hard, semi-sweet cheese from province of Parma, though it in fact originated in the Enza valley, between Parma nd Reggio); also called *grana* (meaning grain and denoting simply a hard, coarse-textured, crumbly type of cheese, of which real Parmesan is the finest)

parrozzo a rich chocolate cake, speciality of the Abruzzi-Molise area

passato purée; *di legume*, vegetable consommé; *di patate*, puréed potatoes

passatelli dumplings; *alla bolognese* (Bologna-style), made with egg dough, cheese, breadcrumbs and beef marrow and cooked in consommé; *in brodo*, made with egg dough, cheese and spinach and cooked in consommé

pasta (1) 'paste', pastry or dough of flour and water, used to make various types of noodles; generic name for various types and shapes of pasta; *asciutta* (dry), generic term for pasta served plain or with a sauce; *in brodo*, served as part of a soup; *e fagioli* (and beans), a thick Venetian soup; *frolla*, sweet shortcrust pastry; *con sarde*, with sardines, Sicilian speciality; *all'uovo*, egg pasta, made with egg as well as flour and water: (2) cake

pastella batter for deep frying

pasticceria pastry

pasticciata (Verona), meat stew; (Milan), a polenta dish baked *au gratin*

pasticciera, crema custard cream made with sugar, eggs, milk, flour and lemon, used for dessert dishes

pasticcio (1) pie, baked dish with pastry crust; *di anolini*, pie made with *pasta frolla* and *anolini*, once a special Sunday dish in Parma; *di maccheroni all'anziana* (Anzio pie), pie containing spaghetti and minced beef or veal, grated orange peel and cinamon, sometimes served with a meat sauce; *di maccheroni alla romana*, dessert dish, Roman-style, made with *rigatoni*, chicken livers, beef, mushrooms and gravy, *pasticciera* cream and *pasta frolla*: (2) pâte; *di fegato di maiale*, pork liver

pastiera Neapolitan cake filled with cottage cheese and candied fruit; *napoletana*, Neapolitan Christmas speciality made of puff pastry with buttermilk and candied fruit

pastina small pasta for soup

pastorella soft cheese, similar to *bel paese*

patate potatoes; *fritte*, fried; *al latte*, cooked in milk; *lesse*, boiled; *purée*, mashed

pavese see *zuppa*

pecorino (romano) Italy's oldest cheese, sharp, hard and white and made from sheep's milk; used in country districts instead of Parmesan; served with pears in Abruzzi region; *sardo*, Sardinian version

pelati peeled plum tomatoes

penne ('feathers'), type of pasta cut in short pieces

peòci mussels (Venetian name); *risotto di*, risotto with; *zuppa di*, soup

pepe pepper; *nero*, black; *rosso*, red

peperata sauce made of beef marrow, butter, breadcrumbs, Parmesan and stock, to accompany *bollito* or cooked hot or cold meat or poultry (speciality of Verona)

peperonata stew made with sweet peppers and tomatoes

peperoni sweet peppers, green (*verdi*), yellow (*gialli*) or red (*rossi*); *ripieni*, stuffed

peperoncini dried or fresh hot red peppers

perciatelli type of pasta, a thinner version of *maccaroncelli*

pere pears; *al forno caramellata*, baked, and served with the caramelized juice; *ripiene*, stuffed, perhaps with gorgonzola cheese or with ground almonds and crystallized fruit

pernici partridges; *arrosto*, roast, stuffed with bacon, ham, mushrooms, juniper berries and the birds' liver; *in brodo*, cooked in broth containing vegetables and basil, served cold with a sauce made with lemon juice and parsley

pesce fish

pesce persico perch, found on the shores on the lake of Maggiore and served wither grilled of fried in fillets or slices

pesce San Pietro John Dory, celebrated in the Veneto region, cooked in various ways

pesce spada swordfish, especially common is Sicily, served grilled, in slice

pesche peaches; *ripiene*, stuffed (with macaroons, egg yolk, sugar and butter); *in vino bianco*, in white wine

pesto (alla genovese) (Genoese) sauce for pasta based on olive oil, in which basil, pine nuts, garlic and both *pecorino* and Parmesan cheese have been steeped; *trenette col*, noodles with

pettirossi robins

petto di pollo chicken breast; *alla bolognese* (Bologna-style), fried, with Parmesan cheese and ham

petto di vitello breast of veal; *arrotolato*, stuffed

pevarada sauce made with lemon, oil and vinegar, garlic, anchovies, chicken livers, grated Parmesan cheese, pepper and ginger, served with game and roast meats

piccate small, thin slices of fried veal, usually moistened with marsala and seasoned with lemon juice (same as *scaloppine*)

piccante piquant

pignolata Neapolitan pastry balls containing lemon and orange peel and dipped in honey

pignoli pine nuts

pimiento red sweet pepper

pincisgrassi type of pasta, cooked in the oven with cheese and a sauce of meat, gravy and cream (Abruzzi-Molise area); see also *vincisgrassi*

piselli peas; *al guanciale* (on a pillow), with fat pork and bacon; *alla toscana* (Tuscan-style), cooked in oil with garlic and bacon; see also *pisellini*

pisellini tiny, very young peas, also called *piselli novelli*; *alla fiorentina* (Florence-style), sautéed with garlic, *prosciutto* and parsley; *al prosciutto*, cooked wtih onions and *prosciutto*, Roman speciality

pizza large circular tart (literally 'pie') with a bread dough base, topped with mozzarella cheese, tomato and a wide variety of other ingredients, including capers, anchovies, marjoram, olives, mushrooms, salami, etc.; *bianco alla romana*, Roman-style, with mozzarella cheese and anchovies; *capricciosa*, topped with anchovies, tomatoes, mussels and mozzarella; *con cozze*, with mussels; *alla francescana*, topped with mushrooms, ham, cheese and tomatoes; *ai funghi*, with mushrooms; *margherita*, with tomatoes, mozzarella and Parmesan cheese; *alla liguria*, see *sardenara*; *alla marinara* (sailor-style), with garlic, tomatoes and olive oil; *napoletana* (Neapolitan), classic version with tomatoes, mozzarella, oregano and anchovies; *pasquale* (Easter), cake made with eggs, ricotta cheese and honey; *alla piemontese* (Piedmont-style), small, filled with tomatoes, peppers and anchovies and served as a starter; *quattro stagioni* ('four seasons'), with four types of topping, such as different cheeses, seafood and other variants on the usual ingredients; *rustica*, made with pastry, filled with a mixture of béchamel sauce, eggs, cheese, ham, salami and hard-boiled eggs, with a pastry top; *sardenara* (Ligurian), with olives, tomatoes, anchovies and onion; *siciliana* (Sicilian-style), with onions, tomato and salami

pizzaiola style of sauce based on tomatoes, garlic and wild marjoram

pizzette small pizzas

pizzichi type of pasta made with egg (same as *farfalline*)

polenta form of semolina made from maize, grown in northern Italy, yellow in colour and eaten either as an accompaniment to a meat dish, or seasoned with a sauce (meat, fish, tomato or mushroom, or combinations), or butter and cheese (e.g. Parmesan); a version of the latter is *polenta grassa* (rich), with layers of *fontina* and butter, wither baked or grilled; *pasticciata*, pie, speciality of Milan; polenta is often served with little birds (*e osei*: a speciality of Bergamo and Brescia)

polipi octopus

polipetti small octopus

pollastro, pollastrino spring chicken

pollo chicken; *all'arrabbiata* ('angry'), braised with vegetables, including hot pepper and tomatoes, in white wine; *arrosto*, roast; *arrosto in tegame*, pot-roasted in white wine with garlic and rosemary; *alla cacciatora* (hunter's-style), braised in wine with mushrooms and tomatoes, sometimes also with green peppers; *alla diavola* ('devilled'), marinated in pepper, oil and lemon and grilled, ideally over charcoal; *finanziera di*, rich chicken mixture in pastry shell (Piedmontese speciality); *fritto*, fried, and served with lemon; *al latte*, cooked in milk; *al limone*, roast with lemon; *con olive*, stewed with vegetables and with olives added to the sauce; *petto di, alla bolognese* (Bologna-style)/*alla fiorentina* (Florence-style)/*alla senese* (Siena-style), breast of, with ham and cheese/fried in butter/with parsley and lemon; *in porchetta*, stuffed with ham and fennel and cooked in butter in the oven; *rollatini di petto di, e maiale*, filleted breast of, stuffed with pork; *tonnato*, served cold with tuna sauce; *in umido con cipolla*, stew with onion

polpette meatballs or rissoles; *alla pizzaiola*, made with beef, cooked with tomatoes, mozzarella and anchovies

polpetti sea stawberries, rosy-coloured baby squid (same as *fragoline di mare* and *moscardini*)

polpettine small meatballs; *di baccalà*, made with salt cod; *alla fiorentina* (Florence-style) with artichokes; *di melanzane*, fried aubergines patties

polpettone meat loaf, or large meat roll containing stuffing; *di tono*, of tuna; *alla toscana* (Tuscan-style), braised in wine with dried mushrooms

pomodori tomatoes; *al forno*, baked; *fritti*, fried; *coi gamberetti*, stuffed with prawns; *di mare*, stuffed with seafood; *minestra di*, soup; *alla siciliana* (Sicilian-style), baked, with anchovies, tuna and black olives; *col tonno*, stuffed with tuna; *zuppa crema di*, cream of, soup

pompelmo grapefruit

porchetta whole sucking pig, served spit-roasted in Umbria and the Marches

porri leeks; *al burro e fromaggio*, braised with Parmesan; *minestra di*, soup; *torta di, e patate*, and potato pie

potacchio special stew or sauce; *anconetano* (from Ancona in the Marches), containing olive oil, white wine, garlic, tomatoes and herbs, served with all sorts of meat, poultry and fish

European Menu Guide

poveracce, poverasse clams

prezzemolo parsley

prosciutto salted, air-cured, uncooked ham (not smoked), speciality of province of Parma; *di cinghiale*, of wild boar; *cotto*, cooked (boiled); *di San Daniele*, Venetian variety of *prosciutto*

provatura, provola buffalo-milk cheese from Campania; *affumicata*, smoked, eaten with good olive oil and freshly ground pepper after the cheese's skin has been removed

provinciale provincial, regional (cooking)

provolone a piquant, semi-hard, creamy cheese that appears in various forms and sizes and may be made from either buffalo's or cow's milk

punta (di vitello arrosto) breast (of veal, roasted)

punti tips (e.g. of asparagus)

puntino, (cotto) al '(cooked) to the exact point', medium-rare (of steak)

purè, purea purée; *di patate*, mashed potatoes (with Parmesan cheese)

purée mashed, puréed

quadrucci ('little squares'), type of pasta made from cross-cut *tagliatelle* and used mainly in soups

quagliata curds, rennet

quaglie quails; *con piselli*, with peas, speciality of Capri

quagliette di vitello slices of veal wraped round ham or other stuffing

radicchio radish; *rosso* (red), winter salad of Trieste area

rafano horseradish; *salsa verde al*, green sauce with

ragù (alla bolognese) meat and tomato sauce for pasta which originated in Bologna; *di funghi*, made with mushrooms; *alla pommarola*, a Neapolitan version made with tomatoes

rane frogs; *in brodo al riso*, dish made with frogs, onions, leeks and various herbs, with rice cooked in the liquid in which these were boiled; *dorate*, skinned, dipped in egg and fried in olive oil (*frittura di*), frogs' legs, treated in the same way), both specialities of Piedmont

rape turnips

rape rosse beetroots

ravioli type of pasta, squares stuffed with meat, vegetables (e.g. spinach) and cheese; *di spinaci e ricotta*, spinach and ricotta dumplings, also known as *gnocchi del casentino*

raviggiolo sheep's milk cheese made in Tuscany and Umbria

razza skate

ricotta soft, bland sheep's-milk cheese made from whey, akin to cottage cheese and much used in Emilia. It is eaten with sugar or cinnamon or salt and used a great deal in cooking

rigatoni type of pasta, ribbed, tubular macaroni, very popular in Florence served with veal *ragù*

ripieno filling, stuffing

riso rice; *arrosto alla genovese* (Genoa-style), timbale of sausage, vegetables and cheese, oven-baked; *in bianco*, boiled, also, in the Veneto, a soup (rice in consommé); *e ceci*, with chick peas, highly spiced and served in a tomato sauce; *al limone*, boiled, with lemon; *alla piemontese* (Piedmont-style), with white truffles

risi e bisi rice and peas (Venetian dish – sometimes listed under soups)

risotto rice cooked in butter with onions, with the addition of stock and white wine (*bianco*); *bianco* (in the Veneto) with fish; *alla certosina* (Carthusian-style), with prawns, mushrooms, peas and tomatoes; *di mare*, with seafood such as lobster and prawn; *alla marinara* (sailor-style), with clams; *alla milanese*, with saffron, which colours the dish deep yellow (classic accompaniment for *osso buco*); *di mitili*, with mussels; *alla paesana* (country-style), with early peas, courgettes and carrots; *di pesce, di pesse*, with fish; *primavera*, with spring vegetables; *alla sbirriglia*, with chicken cut into small pieces; *alla toscana* (Tuscan-style), with pot-roast, mushrooms and tomatoes; *alla veronese* (Verona-style), with ham, in mushroom sauce

ristretto concentrated

robiola soft, runny, white, full-flavoured cow's-milk cheese from Lombardy

robiolina more powerful variety of *robiola*

rognoncini kidneys; *trifolati*, sautéed, sliced lamb or veal kidneys

rolé roll; *di manzo*, beef; *di vitello*, veal

rotolini small rolls; *di vitello al pomodoro*, veal rolls with
tomato sauce

romano see *pecorino*

rosmarino rosemary

rossa red; *salsa*, sauce of onions, tomatoes and green
peppers, with a little chilli, served warm with various meat
dishes, including *bollito misto*

rotelle type of pasta, usually served with *ragú*

sagnettine type of pasta, otherwise known as *linguine*

salame salami, spiced pork sausage (speciality of Bologna) of
which many varieties exist, some strongly flavoured with
garlic

salamoia brine

sale salt

salmi stewed in wine and other ingredients (see *lepre*);
classic Tuscan mode of cooking game

salmone salmon

salsa sauce; *genovese*, Genoese, made with veal, various
vegetables, tomatoes and wine; *di pomodoro*, tomato,
including also vegetables and meat; *di pomodoro al marsala*,
with tomatoes, ham or bacon, garlic and Marsala; *piccante*,
piquant, with red wine, oil, vinegar, herbs and garlic

salsiccia fresh spiced sausage

saltato sautéed

saltimbocca ('jump into the mouth'), a popular Roman dish
consisting of slices of veal fillet rolled in ham, fried in butter,
flavoured with sage and sprinkled with Marsala wine

salvia sage

sangue, al rare (of steak)

sanguinaccio creamy dessert flavoured with chocolate
(Neapolitan speciality)

saraghine sardines (dialect word); *alla brace* (embers),
grilled

sarde, sardelle sardines (in Italy mainly fresh, not tinned); *in
carpione*, fried and marinated with garlic and vegetables
(Lombardy name: also known as *in saor* in the Veneto
region and a *scapece* in Sicily), served without re-heating;
ripiene, stuffed with bread and Parmesan cheese and fried

savoiarda meat-and-fish salad, speciality of Monza, with
calf's-head meat, boiled pork, tongue, tuna fish, anchovies,

various pickles, capers, parsley and pickled yellow and red peppers

savoiardi sponge fingers (used in *zuppa inglese*)

scaloppe, scaloppine escalopes; small, thin slices (of veal, usually), often served moistened with Marsala and seasoned with lemon juice (see *piccate*)

scampi scampi (shrimps); *fritti*, fried; *alla griglia*, grilled; *alle stecche*, on skewers; *in umido*, stewed

scarole small, Batavian endives

scarpaccia ('big old shoe'), sort of large pizza made in Tuscany with courgettes, onion and Parmesan cheese

schie clams

scottiglia stew, usually incorporating pieces of bread

secco dry

sedano celery

selvaggina game

semolina cereal, the finely ground heart of the wheat

senapa mustard

sepolini squid

seppie cuttle-fish

sfinciuni double pizza, speciality of Palermo, with two layers of dough enclosing the stuffing, or *conzo* (e.g. tomato, onion and anchovy, or ricotta cheese and broccoli); *di San Vito*, with a stuffing of beef, ham, onion, breadcrumbs and *fontina* and ricotta cheese

sfinge (di San Giuseppe) Sicilian pastry flavoured with orange peel and made by monks

sfoglia flaky (of pastry)

sfogliatelle fan-shaped pastry filled with sweetened ricotta cheese and candied fruit, speciality of Naples

sformato mould; *di spinaci*, spinach

soffiato soufflé; *di gamberi*, prawn

soffrito a spicy base for soups, sauces and meat dishes

sogliola sole; *al marsala*, browned in butter and splashed with Marsala and fish broth; *alla parmigiana*, browned in butter and topped with Parmesan cheese

soppresse pork and beef salami, speciality of Verona

sorbetto sorbet

spada swordfish

spaghetti type of pasta; *arrabbiata* ('angry'), with pimentos and tomatoes; *bolognese* (Bologna-style), with meat sauce (*ragù*) and Parmesan; *a cacio e pepe*, with *pecorino* and pepper; *alla carbonara*, with eggs, bacon (ideally *pancetta*) and Parmesan; *alla prestinara*, with only garlic and oil; *alla siciliana* (Sicilian-style), with aubergines and ricotta cheese

spalla di vitello brasata shoulder of veal braised in white wine

spec smoked raw ham, a version of *prosciutto* found in the Dolomite region

spigola sea bass, usually served roasted or grilled (known as *branzino* on Adriatic coast)

spinaci spinach; *sformato di*, mould

spuma mousse

spumone a frozen cream similar to ice-cream (speciality of Naples)

stecche, alle on small sticks, skewered

stelline ('little stars'), type of minature pasta for soups

stoccafisso stockfish or salt cod (same as *baccalà*)

storione sturgeon, fairly common on the Adriatic coast, usually served oven-roasted or cooked over charcoal

stracchino soft cow's-milk cheese, similar to *taleggio*

stracci type of pasta, irregular in shape, served with a sauce of tomato and pieces of mutton, also known as *carte da guioco* (card-game)

stracciatella ('little rags'), soup made with meat broth, beaten eggs and Parmesan (Roman speciality)

stracotto ('overcooked', long-cooked), pot-roast (especially beef); *al Barolo*, beef braised in red wine; *alla fiorentina*, Florentine beef stew cooked in chianti

strangolapreti, strangolaprieviti ('priest-straglers'), type of pasta, dumplings containing cheese, egg and pieces of bacon; also known as *gnocchetti cacio e ova*

stufato ('smothered'), stew; *manzo, al vino rosso*, beef, in red wine; *di manzo alla genovese*, Genoese beef, with vegetables and white wine

stufatino stew; *alla romana*, Roman-style, made with beef, bacon, marjoram and red wine

succutundu Sardinian dish, a highly concentrated *bouillon* containing balls of semolina

suffli soufflé; light, frothy, baked egg dish

sugo sauce (particularly for pasta), juice; *di carne*, meat sauce, incorporating onion, carrot, celery, dried mushrooms and wine; *di pomodoro*, tomato juice

supplì rice croquettes, also containing *mortadell*a sausage (or ham) and cheese; *al telefono* 'telephone croquettes', containing buffalo-milk cheese (*provatura* or *mozzarella*) that hangs down like telephone wires when the croquette is bitten

tacchino turkey; *arrosto ripieno*, roast, and stuffed with its own liver, veal, chestnuts, Parmesan cheese and prunes; *stufato al vino bianco*, braised, in white wine

taccozzelle type of pasta, rectangular in shape, served with cottage cheese and tomato sauce

tagliarini alternative name for *tagliolini*

tagliatelle type of pasta cut into thin strips (ribbon egg noodles); *alla bolognese or al ragù*, served with special meat sauce devised in Bologna; *al pesto*, with pesto sauce; *al ragù*, same as *alla bolognese*

tagliolini type of pasta, thinner version of *tagliatelle*

taleggio mild, creamy cow's-milk cheese from Lombardy

taleggino stronger variety of *taleggion*

tartufi truffles; *bianchi*, white; *di mare*, sea, served raw; *neri*, black

te tea

telline clams (Florentine name) or mussels

tomini del talucco a goat's-milk cheese made in Piedmont, at Pinado

tonnarelle type of pasta, cut thin; *alla paesana* (country-style), served with a *ragù* containing mushrooms and bacon

tonnellini type of pasta, very fine homemade egg noodle; *con funghi e piselli*, with mushrooms and peas

tonno tuna or tunny fish; *salsa di*, hot sauce containing also parsley and butter

topinambur Jerusalem artichokes; *gratinati*, *gratiné*e, with a Parmesan topping; *insalata di*, *e spinaci*, and spinach salad; *trifolati*, sautéed

tordi thrushes

torrone nougat, speciality of Cremona; *molle*, soft, a sweet made with cocoa, sugar, butter, eggs, plain biscuits and ground almonds

torta (sweet) tart, flan, cake, pie; *pasqualina*, elaborate (Genoese) Easter pie made with leeks or artichokes, curds, grated cheese, milk, olive oil and eggs in a puff-pastry case; *di riso*, sweet rice cake, Easter speciality of Bologna

tortellini type of pasta, resembling tiny hats and stuffed with a pork, egg, cheese and spice mixture, served either with a *ragù* or in a soup

tortelloni type of pasta, large squares usually served stuffed with Swiss chard or spinach; *di biete*, stuffed with Swiss chard; *al burro e formaggio*, cooked with butter and Parmesan

tortiglione almond cakes

tortiglioni type of pasta, similar to the corkscrew-shaped *fusilli*

tortino di carciofi eggs with artichokes, Florentine speciality

totani long-boiled squid; *al prezzemole*, with parsley

trenette type of pasta, Genoa's name for thin ribbon noodles, same as *tagliolini*; see also *pesto*

tremezzini sandwiches

triglie red mullet, speciality of Livorno; *gravide*, 'pregnant', stuffed with a mixture of *prosciutto* and parsley; *alla livornese* (Livorno-style), with tomato sauce

trionfo di gola ('triumph of the palate'), acclaimed Sicilian sweet made by monks to a secret recipe

trippa tripe; *alla fiorentina* (Florence-style), with tomato sauce and Parmesan cheese; *alla parmigiana*, fried; *marinata all'arancio*, marinated with orange and served cold

tubetti type of pasta, same as *ditalini*

tufoli type of pasta, giant stuffed macaroni tubes

ubriaco 'drunken' (usually, cooked in wine)

uccelletti small birds, such as thrushes, larks, blackbirds, robins and bullfinches, served roasted or grilled, with *polenta* (in northern Italy), *migliaccio* and/or rice; *scappati* ('escaped'), slices of veal wrapped round ham or other stuffing

uova egg; *alla cocca*, boiled; *alla fiorentina* (Florence-style), oven-baked dish of poached eggs on buttered spinach;

sode in salsa verde, hard-boiled, with green sauce

uva grapes; *nera,* black

uva spina gooseberry

valdostana in the style of the Val d'Aosta

valligiana, alla in the style of the valley (local version)

vaniglia vanilla

ventresca tuna fish

verde green (usually denoting spinach); *salsa*, sauce, made with parsley, capers and anchovies, classic accompaniment for *bollito misto* and various fish and meat dishes

verdure vegetables or greens

vermicelli type of pasta, very fine spaghetti used in soups

verza savoy cabbage

vincisgrassi name used in the Marches, where it originated, for the baked pasta dish *pincisgrassi*

vitello veal; tonnato, sliced with tuna sauce, a classic cold dish

vongole shellfish, cockles or clams (southern Italian name)

zabaglione, zabaione egg and Marsala sauce; also frothy dessert dish (containing sugar in addition), served warm in glasses

zafferano saffron

zampa (calf's) leg

zamponi pigs' trotters, a speciality of Modena, which are stufed with seasoned pork, boiled for several hours and served, thickly sliced, with *salsa verde* or mustard

zemino see *zimino*

zeppole sweet made of honey, dried figs, almonds and other nuts, speciality of the Abruzzi-Molise region; *alla napoletana* (Naples-style), brandy-flavoured fritters; *di San Giuseppe*, cinnamon-flavoured fritters, shaped like a ring doughnut, sold from street stalls (speciality for St Joseph's Day)

zimino fish stew; see *lumache*

ziti type of pasta, large tubes of macaroni

zucca pumpkin; *cappellacci di*, pasta filled with (speciality of Ferrara)

zucchine/zucchini courgettes, baby marrows; *frittata di*, omelette with courgettes; fritte, fried battered slices; *della nonna* (grandmother's), fried in oil with the addition of beated egg and grated Parmesan

zuccotto rich Florentine dessert made with sponge cake, cocoa, chocolate, liqueur and spirits

zuppa soup; *alla certosina* (Carthusian-style), breaded vegetable; *di cozze*, mussel; *di datteri*, with shellfish (sea dates, found off the Genoese coast); *di frutti di mare*, seafood; *alla genovese*, fish; *di granchi*, crab; *inglese* (see below); *di lenticchie*, lentil; *di mitili*, mussel; *alla pavese* (Pavia-style), hot broth poured over eggs on slices of toast; *di peòci*, Venetian mussel; *di pesce*, fish; *di pomodoro*, tomato; *primavera*, spring vegetable; *reale*, royal, with separate egg yolks and whites (Abruzzi speciality); *di vercolore*, green soup, with vegetables, herbs and watercress; *di verdure*, vegetable; *di congole*, clam

zuppa inglese trifle, decorated with whipped cream and crystallized fruit

Spain

Spain's cuisine – or *cocina*, to use the right language – is surely the most underrated in Europe. The package holiday boom has introduced several generations of holidaymakers from other European countries – and especially and notoriously Britain – to the doubtful delights of *paella*, *sangría* and *filete con patatas*. Doubtful they are because the British visitors did not demand high standards, only sunshine. As a result, all too many restaurateurs understandably fobbed the masses off with *paella* which was all rice and no tasty bits, *sangría* which was no better than cheap lemonade, and miserable pieces of meat with the ubiquitous chip.

But all these items *can* be delights if you avoid the tourist traps and recognise that the food of Spain has to be taken on its own terms. It is perhaps the most distinctive and uncompromising of the European cuisines. While you can create an authentic *coq au vin* – to take another much-maligned dish – at home, the simple *tortilla* will elude you. Though you may have brought home the oil from your holiday in Spain, there will be something about the potatoes and the onions that will not taste the same. Or is it simply that a *tortilla* can only be enjoyed in a bar as a *tapa*, with a chilled glass of *fino*, or a refreshing draught beer?

The other key to the cuisine is knowing how to put a meal together, and that is where it is uncompromising. A humble *filete con patatas* eaten at 2.30pm or 3.00pm after a first course of a fresh mixed salad, preceded by several beers and some tantalising tapas earlier in the day, and followed by fresh fruit or homemade flan is a far cry from that miserable piece of steak and two veg that it becomes back home at 1.00pm.

So if you have enjoyed the dish of mixed dried fish that is so popular in Andalusia, recreate it at home (even though the fish will be far less varied and probably frozen). But don't serve it with fried potatoes or vegetables on the same plate. Serve an *ajo blanco* garnished with grapes to start with, make a salad of lettuce, tomato and onion dressed in oil and wine vinegar, and make sure you have plenty of good fresh white bread to mop up the juicy bits.

The bread is really indispensable, bought fresh every day. Take one of the simple egg dishes — eggs baked in tomato sauce that also contains asparagus tips, ham, artichoke hearts and peas. First dip your bread to soak up all the juices. Poached eggs on toast were never as enjoyable as this.

This egg dish is a very likely supper dish, since lunch is for most the main meal of the day. The evening meal starts at around 9.00: a little earlier in the winter, much later in the height of summer. In good weather the early evening is too good to spend indoors eating; you will be out on the main street or in a cool avenue parading in your best clothes, and perhaps enjoying an ice cream, a small cake or a drink, depending on your age and appetite.

Spain's fruit and vegetable growers are very successful at growing produce throughout the European winter; the southerly latitude of the Canaries helps here. What Spain lacks, though, is good pasture, and what it gains in horticultural produce and in fish it loses in meat. That's why you will find little beef steak on the menu, and why there are so many recipies for using up every part of the animal that is available. Nothing can be wasted when the meat is so precious.

The best of the meat dishes can be found in northern Spain, which enjoys a generally richer and more varied diet. While the French have a rigorous practice of giving the same name to the same sauce, the Spaniards are more relaxed. However, there are some general guidelines. If you find a dish labelled *a la catalana*, or *vizcaina*, or *barcelonesa*, you will probably find that it contains peppers of the sweet and the chili variety, in addition to tomatoes, and may well also contain one of the many sausages in which Spain abounds.

Recipes from Valencia are very likely to contain oranges or

almonds, while those from Seville usually contain tomatoes, onions, garlic and olives. Those from Jerez, of course, contain sherry. Apart from some classic dishes, though, there is great variation, so if in doubt, ask.

You will never be at a loss for something sweet to nibble in Spain, though the quality varies. Nothing can beat the *turrones* of Alicante and Jijona, the marzapanes of Toledo, and the *yemas*. But if you have a taste for something savoury instead, then you will not be disappointed. Shops and market stalls everywhere sell a vast range of nuts and fried, salted beans, and round every corner you will find a shop with a vast vat of oil that makes sweet *churros* in the morning, and fresh crisp, crisps in the afternoon. It's all too easy to get fat in Spain, so make sure you plan some vigorous sightseeing.

Note:

In Spanish the letter of the alphabet Ch follows C and Ll follows L, but for convenience's sake the two have been combined in this book. Any traveller to Spain who takes an interest in fish should be sure to take Alan Davidson's indispensable *Mediterranean Seafood* with them to help identify the vast range of fish on offer, especially in coastal towns and villages.

Phrases For The Restaurant

I want to reserve a table for.....at .....
Quiero reservar una mesa para.....a las ....

Have you a table for.....
Tiene una mesa para.....

A quiet table
Una mesa al lado de la ventana

A table on the terrace
Una mesa en la terraza por favor

Could we have another table please?
¿Podemos elegir otra mesa por favor?

I am in a hurry/we are in a hurry
Tengo prisa/Tenemos prisa

Please bring me the menu
Por favor puede traerme el menú

Can we have ..... please
Podemos tener un ..... por favor

Local dishes
Las especialidades de la región

How much is it?
¿Cuanto cuesta?

What is it?
¿Que es esto?

I did not order this
Yo no he pedido esto

Too much
Demasiado

More
Mas (por favor)

The bill please
La cuenta por favor

Is service included?
¿Està el servicio includio?

I think there is a mistake in the bill
Creo que hay una equivocación en la cuenta

Do you accept travellers' cheques?
¿Acepta usted cheques de viajero?

Restaurant Terms

abierto

open

el almuerzo

lunch

basta

enough

la barra

the bar – it is usually cheaper to eat at the bar than at the table, la mesa; sitting outside is generally most expensive of all – by law, every bar has its price list publicly displayed and and this will show the differential between bar, table and table outside.

bien hecho

well cooked (of steak)

bodega

a place where wine, particularly sherry, is made

bodegón

a small bar-cum-restaurant

la caja

till, cash desk

camerero

waiter

carnes

the meat section of the menu

la carta

the menu

de la casa

of the house, homemade

la cena

dinner

un cenicero

ash tray

cerrado

closed; festivos, closed on public holidays

cerillas

matches

cigarillos

cigarettes; the rubio or 'blond' kind are mild, the negro or 'black' are stronger

el comedor

dining room

comida

meal, lunch

confiteria, reposteria, pasteleria

cake shop

un cuchillo

a knife

la cuenta

bill

cubitos

ice cubes

una cuchara

spoon

el desayuno

breakfast

ensaladas

salads

especialidad de la casa

speciality of the house

fritos

fried dishes

guiso, guisado/a(s)

stew, stewed

el menú

menu; del día, fixed price menu. Usually consists of soup or other entremeses, meat or fish, dessert, bread and a quarter of a litre of table wine; turístico, a meal selected from the various groups on the menu

otro/a(s)

another, other

plato del día

dish of the day; plato combinado, a complete meal on one plate, a picture of which is usually displayed on the walls of the café or bar

prohibido

forbidden; fumar, no smoking

una ración

a portion of food

ristorante
restaurant
salida
exit; de socorro, emergency exit
sencillo/a(s)
simple
servicio incluido
service included
servicios
lavatories
sopas
soups
una taza
a cup (of tea etc.)
un tenedor
a fork
tengo prisa
I'm in a hurry; tenemos prisa, we're in a hurry
variado/a(s)
varied, mixed
un vaso
glass, (for wine, water)
venta
roadside bar often providing good simple meals

Menu Terms

abadejo fish of the grouper family

acedera(s) sorrel

acedías baby soles, often served *fritas*, fried, from Andalucia

aceite oil; *de olivia*, olive oil; *de girasol*, sunflower seed oil

acentunas olives; there are three grades: the finest is the small *manzanilla*, next, the large *gordal del rey* or 'queen', and finally the small *hoji blanca*: they are often sold in markets *en ajo*, pickled with oil, vinegar and garlic

acelgas chard; *torta de acelga*, a form of quiche

adobo marinade

adorno garnish

agua water; *con gas*, sparkling; *sin gas*, still; *mineral*, mineral; *potable*, drinking

aguacate avocado pear

aguiat a way of cooking meat with onions and garlic in oil and stock very slowly until the liquid evaporates, from Mallorca

aguija beef blade

ahumado smoked

ajo garlic; blanco, a cold soup of almonds and garlic often garnished with white grapes, from Malaga; *revuelto de ajos*, scrambled eggs with tender garlic shoots

ajo harina 'garlic flour': *bacalao* or dried salt cod baked on a bed of potatoes in garlic, tomato and pepper sauce thickened with flour

ajonjoli sesame

ala wing (of game and poultry)

alacha a member of the sardine family

albaricoque apricot

albondigas meat balls; *de pescado*, fish balls

alcachofa artichoke; *con vinagreta*, with vinaigrette dressing; *fondo de –*, hearts; *con atún*, with tuna fish in vinaigrette or mayonnaise

alcaparra caper

algarroba carob bean

algas seaweed

all-i-oli/ali-oli garlic and oil sauce, served with meat, fish and vegetables particularly in Catalonia

almeja clam

almendras almonds; *tostadas*, toasted, served as a *tapa*

almondiguilles meatballs of minced veal and sobresada, in a sauce finished with a hot, garlicky *picada*

almíbar syrup; *melocotones en almíbar*, peaches in syrup, usually peach halves

alubias kidney beans

amargo bitter

amettles grilled almonds covered in chocolate or praline, a Catalan recipe

anchoas or boquerones anchovies; these are often dipped in flour and deep fried with their tails joined in the form of a fan; *en cazuela*, dish of layered onions and anchovies, sprinkled with oil and paprika

anec amb figues duck stuffed with minced veal and pork, in a sauce to which dried figs are added near the end of cooking

angelote monkfish

anguila eel; *al horno*, baked with white wine, tomatoes, onions, potatoes and almonds, from Catalonia

angulas baby eels or elvers, cooked in oil and garlic in a small earthenware dish and eaten with a wooden fork

apio celery

arenques herrings; *ahumados*, smoked; *en adobo*, marinated in a wine vinegar marinade

arroz rice; most of the made-up rice dishes are variants of *paella*, with the ingredients depending on the cook, the region and what's in season; *a la marinera*, with fish, from Valencia; *a la mallorquina*, with pigeon, mussels, fish and sobresada; *con bacalao*, with salt cod and mussels, a Basque recipe; *con huevos*, a rice dish served with rice-stuffed tomatoes, hard-boiled eggs and tomato sauce; *con mahonesa*, cold rice with mayonnaise, sometimes with fish or vegetables, from Andalucia; *a banda*, with fish, from Valencia; *arroz con leche*, a sweet rice pudding

asado/a(s) roast

atún tuna; *encebollado*, baked with onions, tomatoes and garlic; *con tomates*, fried and then served with a thick sauce of tomatoes, onion, garlic, and white wine; *a la brasa*, marinated in oil and vinegar, then grilled and served with a tomato sauce

avellana hazelnut

avena oat

aves poultry

azafrán saffron; gives the distinctive colour to *paella*

azúcar sugar

bacalao dried salt cod; *al pil-pil*, with olie oil, garlic and hot peppers, a Basque recipe; *a la vizcaína*, in a sauce of hot red peppers, tomatoes, onions and garlic, a Basque recipe; *a la gallega*, with green and red peppers and shallots; *en ajo arrier*, fried with garlic, tomatoes and red peppers, to which beated eggs are added, from Old Castile; *buñuelos de bacalao*, fritters of *bacalao*, also known as *tortillitas*

baila a form of the bass family

barquillo ice-cream cone

batatas sweet potatoes; *confitadas*, cooked and dipped in syrup, as a sweet

un batido a milk shake

becada woodcock

berenjena(s) aubergine(s); *a la plancha*, cooked whole on a hot plate, then peeled and served with olive oil; *rellenas*, stuffed with veal, cheese and onions, from Menorca

berro watercress

berza andaluza a stew of mixed meat and vegetables

besugo red bream; *al horno*, baked with garlic, parsley, pine kernels and wine, often served at Christmas Eve; *a la donostiarra*, 'San-Sebastian-style', grilled with a garlic and chilli sauce; *al ajoarriero*, with garlic, parsley and onions

bistec steak; the lack of good pasture means that most of the calves are killed off young and eaten as veal; beef steak in uncommon and not always reliable; *bien hecho*, well done; *no muy hecho*, medium; *poco hecho*, rare

bizcocho sponge cake, which comes in many varieties; *de San Lorenzo*, with chestnut purée and orange flowere water

blanquets pigs' or calves' brains stuffed with herbs, pine kernels and egg yolks, from Mallorca; also the name for small white puddings

bogavante lobster

bolas, bolitas balls, little balls (e.g. of cheese)

bolets Catalan for mushrooms

un bollo a bread roll

bonito bonito – a tuna-like fish

borrachos 'drunken, tipsy', little cakes soaked in syrup and sweet Malaga wine

boga bogue fish; not particularly tasty

borregos unsweetened biscuits for buttering or dipping in coffee, a Catalan recipe

a la brasa braised

brazo de gitano 'Gypsy's arm', a kind of swiss roll

breca pandora fish, a member of the bream family

brochetas kebabs; *de cigalas*, crayfish tails on skewers with onions and peppers, cooked on a charcoal grill

brossat mallorquì a version of a *crema catalana* made with almond milk

brótola de roca forkbeard fish of the cod family

buey ox, beef; *estofado de buey*, stewed beef, with wine, vegetables and herbs

buñuelos fritters

bunyettes a Catalan version of the French beignet, popular at Easter

bunyols small doughnuts, eaten particularly during Holy Week in Catalonia

butifarra a large, fat, pork sausage flavoured with almonds, pine kernels, cinnamon and cumin; comes in two types, *blance* (white) and *negra* (black), the small thin variety are called *butifarrones*, from Catalonia and Mallorca

butifarrones see *butifarra*

caballa mackerel; *a la gaditana* grilled and served with chopped tomato, onion and green pepper, from Cadiz; *con hojas de limonero*, barbecued of a rack covered with lemon leaves, from Catalonia

cabello de angel 'angel's hair', a kind of jam made from the fibrous part of a pumpkin or squash

cabeza head

cabrito kid, from *cabra*, goat

cachelada *chorizo* and potato stew, from Leon

cadera rump

café coffee; *con leche*, white coffee; *solo*, black, expresso coffee; *un descafeinado* is a decaffeinated coffee; *un café cortado*, an almost black coffee

calabacines courgettes; *rellenos*, halved and stuffed with onion, garlic and parsley, topped with cheese and breadcrumbs and baked, also sometimes with a bèchamel sauce; *fritos*, cut into rings and fried; *rebozados y fritos*, dipped in batter and fried

calabaza pumpkin

calamares squid; *en su tinta*, cooked in their ink; *fritos* or *a la romana*, rings deep fried in batter; *rellenos*, stuffed with ham and hard-boiled eggs

calçotada a Catalan dish of grilled onions, served with *romesco* sauce

caldeirada a fish dish like *bouillabaise*, from Galicia

caldera menorquina a fish soup, with tomato, garlic and parsley, from Menorca

caldereta a stew; *asturiana*, of fish and shellfish; *extremeña*, of kid

caldillo de perro 'dog soup'; a soup of small hake with bitter oranges, from Andalucia

caldo broth, consommé; *gallego*, with ham bones, haricot beans and vegetables; *de pescado*, a soup containing a variety of fish

caliente hot

callos tripe; *a la madrileña*, with *morcilla*, *chorizo* and red peppers; *a la asturiana*, with garlic, smoked ham, *chorizo* and hot peppers; *a la catalana*, with tomatoes and potatoes; *a la gallega*, with chick-peas, pig's trotters, paprika and *chorizo*; *a la andaluza*, with chick-peas and calves' feet

camarones prawns

cañadilla the murex, a mollusc with an attractive shell found on the Andalucian coast

canalones cannelloni

canela cinnamon

cangrejo crayfish; *de río*, freshwater crayfish

canaílla a sea snail found on the Andalucian coast, served cold

cap de xaï rostit roasted lamb's head, served with sautéed potatoes, from Catolonia

capirotada meat with almond sauce, from Mallorca

capón capon; *a la vasca*, roast, stuffed with sausage, pork and hazelnuts; *relleno a la andaluza*, stuffed with pine kernels, raisins and sherry; *relleno a la catalana*, stuffed with sausage, portk, pig's ear, peaches, prunes, pine kernels and beans

caqui persimmon or kaki-fruit

caracoles small snails; *de navarra*, with tomatoes, green peppers and chillis

caramelo caramel

carbayones cake made of almonds, sugar and eggs, from Asturias

cardo/cardón cardoon, a celery-like vegetable; *a la navarra*, in a white sauce with ham

cargolada barbecued snails, served with *all-i-oli* and bread, a traditional Catalan dish on Easter Monday

carn amb castanyes beef or veal fried with a *sofregit* or *sofrito* of tomatoes and onions, and a *picada*, a hot, garlicky paste added, then cooked with chestnuts, from Catalonia

carne meat, usually beef; *mechada*, beef casserole; *mechada a la andaluza*, a piece of beef stuffed with olives and almonds; *fiambre*, cold meat, sometimes made into a form of meat loaf, and sliced; *picada*, minced

carnero muton; *estofado de carnero*, pot roasted

casadielles walnut-stuffed fried pastries

cáscara peel (of lemon, orange)

castañas chestnuts; *puré de castañas*, chestnut purée

castellano creamy sheep's milk cheese with a yellow rind, from Old Castile

caza game

cazón baby shark

cazuela a stew; *a la catalana*, of minced beef and sausage, with carrots, onions and tomatoes; *de habas verdes a la granadina*, broad beans with tomatoes and artichokes, with eggs baked on top

cebolla(s) onion(s); *guisadas*, braised; *rellenas*, stuffed

centolla/changurro spider crab; *relleno*, stuffed and baked with a mixture of its own meat, hake, onion, parsley, garlic and lemon juice, with a cheese and breadcrumb topping

cerdo pork; *chuletas*, chops; *lomo*, loin; *manos*, trotters;

pierna, leg; *oreja*, ear

cerezas cherries

cerveza beer

chamfaina a stew of liver, and sometimes also lungs

champán champagne; *cava* is the name given to sparkling wines produced by the *méthode champenoise* in Spain. Most *cava*s sold in Spain are *semi-seco*, medium-sweet to sweet rather than medium dry

champiñón(-ones) mushroom(s)

chanquetes tiny gobies, a fish eaten – like whitebait – deep fried in batter

chilindrón a sauce of onion, peppers, ham, tomatoes, paprika, saffron and hot red peppers, for chicken, pork, lamb or rabbit

chipirones baby squid; *a la plancha*, cooked on a hot plate with garlic and parsley; *rellenos*, stuffed with bacon, garlic, parsley and the tentacles, chopped

chocha woodcock; *a la vizcaína*, with ham, turnips and sherry, a Basque recipe

chocolate chocolate; hot chocolate is often served at breakfast-time, it is very thick and sweet and goes well with churros

chocos squid

chopa black bream

chorizo spicy red sausage of pork, pork fat, paprika and garlic, eaten thinly sliced or in a *bocadillo*, or in stews where it adds a distinctive flavour

chuleta chop; *de cerdo*, pork; *de cordero*, lamb; *de ternera*, veal; *empanadas*, lamb chops dipped in egg and breadcrumbs and fried; *salteadas*, veal chops with wine and mushrooms; *de cordero a la navarra*, in a sauce of tomatoes, onion and ham, topped with *chorizo*; *de cordero a la riojana*, with tomatoes, red peppers and ham, garnished with hard-boiled eggs

churrasco steak grilled over charcoal, from Cordoba

churros traditional dish of crisp tubes of doughnut mixture, coated in sugar, eaten at elevenses with milky coffee or thick chocolate

ciervo deer

cigalas cigales, small, flat lobsters

ciruelas plums

clara de huevo egg white

cloïsses a la planxa a dish from the Costa Brava of clams cooked on a hot plate

coca mallorquina a Mallorcan version of pizza

cochifrito a fricassée of lamb with onions, garlic, paprika, parsley and lemon juice

cochinillo milk-fed sucking pig; *asado*, roast, is a typical dish of Segovia

cocido stew; with many regional variations; *madrileño*, a traditional dish of chick peas, a boiling fowl, beef, bacon, *chorizo*, onions, cabbage and other vegetables – the broth is eaten first, then the drained meats and vegetables

coco coconut

codornices quails

col cabbage

cola tail; *de cangrejo*, crayfish tails

coles de bruselas brussels sprouts

coliflor cauliflower; *al estilo de Badajoz*, the florets are dipped in egg and breadcrumbs and deep-fried; *budín de coliflor*, cauliflower pudding

comino cumin

compota stewed fruit

un coñac a brandy

una concha a shell, usually scallop shells; *mejillones en concha*, mussels served in their half shells

conejo rabbit; *a la valenciana*, with green peppers, garlic and parsley; *a la ampurdana*, with wine and chocolate; *guisado*, stewed with white wine; *en sarmorejo*, marinated in white wine, them baked with garlic, paprika and chilli pepper, from the Canary Islands

confitura jam, more often than not, apricot jam

congelado/a(s) frozen

congre amb panses conger eel in a wine sauce with raisins and croûtons, from Formentra

congrio conger eel

consomé consommé; *al jerez*, with sherry, and usually served with a glass of sherry

copa hela ice-cream sundae

coquinas the wedge shell, a cockle-like mollusc, can be

eaten raw

corazón heart

cordero lamb; *lechazo*, milk-fed baby lamb; *asado*, roast; *al chilindrón*, with bacon, red peppers and tomatoes; *al ajillo pastor*, with white wine, paprika, garlic and saffron, served with fried potatoes; *en menestra*, with carrots, peas and artichokes

corona crown

corvina meagre fish, resembles sea bass

corzo roe deer

costillas ribs, spare-ribs; *de cordero con all-i-oli*, grilled ribs of lamb with garlic sauce

crema (1) a smooth soup or purée; (2) a sweet smooth dessert; *crema catalana*, a variation on flam with a burnt sugar topping and a popular dessert in Catalonia; (3) a sweet cream filling for cakes

criadillas fritas fried bull's testicles

croquetas croquettes, usually of ham and pork, or chicken, in a thick white sauce which is shaped into croquettes dipped in egg and breadcrumbs and deep-fried

crudo/a(s) raw

cuajada junket

dátil(-es) date(s)

despojos offal

dorada gilt-head bream

dulce (adj.) sweet; *dulce malagueño*, a dessert of semolina, egg yolks, sugar, raisins and *membrillo*

empanada a large, flat, savoury pie, served in wedges, or as individual pies (often known as *empanadillas*), stuffed with meat or fish, from Galicia

empanado/a(s) in breadcrumbs

empedrat Catalan salad of *bacalao*, onions, tomatoes, olives, garlic, haricot beans in vinaigrette

endivias chicory; *al graten*, chicory *au gratin*

ensaimadas a light bun, usually filled with whipped cream, from Mallorca

ensalada salas; *mixta*, mixed, usually lettuce, tomatoes and onions in vinaigrette; *de tomate*, tomatoes and onions in vinaigrette; *rusa*, Russian salad of mayonnaise mixed with cold, cooked potatoes, carrots, peas, peppers, olives, etc.

often displayed in a large mound in bars, and served with bread as a tapa; *de arroz*, rice salad, of rice with vegetables such as peas, peppers, tomatoes with vinaigrette; *sevillana*, of olives, onions, peppers and tomatoes in vinaigrette.

ensucrats de tarragona almond-flavoured cigar-shaped biscuits

entremeses *hors d'oeuvres*; usually the first course of a meal, in contrast to *tapas*

escabeche marinade

escalivada Catalan salad of baked aubergines, onions and tomatoes sprinkled with oil and seasoning, served cold in a vinaigrette – may also contain meat

escudella i carn d'olla a typical Catalan dish which varies from cook to cook; the first part is a soup, the second a plate of veal, pork, chicken, blood sausage and vegetables, it also contains a *pelota*, a large meat ball

espada, pez espada swordfish; often served simply fried, or baked, *al horno*, in wine and seasoning, or marinaded and then grilled, *a la parrillaq*

espadín sprat

espaldilla shoulder (e.g. of lamb)

espárragos asparagus; *puntas de espárragos*, tips

espinacas spinach; *a la catalana*, with pine kernels and raisins

esqueixada vinaigrette of dried salt cod, from Catalonia

al etilo de in the style of

estofado stewed; *de buey*, beef stew

estofat a Catalan dish of marinated meat – veal, beef, hare, rabbit – cooked very slowly with onions, tomatoes and vegetables, and a little wine; the meat is cooked in its own juice

estragon tarragon

fabada a stew from Astiroas (*Fabada asturiana*) but eated widely; based on white beans, flavoured with *morcilla*, *chorizo* and *tocino*, as well as pig's trotters, salt beef and vegetables

faisan pheasant

fava i fideus soup of broad beans and vermicelli, from Menorca

faves broad beans, also more generally known as *habas*; *a la* *catalana*, with pork ribs and *butifarra*

fideos vermicelli; *a la catalana*, pork ribs in tomato sauce with *butifarrones* and vermicelli

fideuà vermicelli with fish, from Valencia

filete fillet

filloas thick, light pancakes, usually filled with jam

flameado flaming, *flambéd*

flan the ubiquitous dessert in restaurants, caramel custard. Make sure that it is home-made and not one of the many commercial varieties; *de queso*, savoury cheese mould

flaó a form of custard tart, eaten at Easter in the Balearics

fondo bottom (e.g. of artichokes)

frambuesas raspberries

frangollos pancakes from the Canary Islands

fresas strawberries

frío cold

frit mallorquí the Mallorcan version of *leche frita*

frito/a(s) fried

frutas fruit; *en almíbar*, in syrup; *de aragón*, candied fruit in chocolate, a speciality of Aragón; *del tiempo*, fresh fruit, of the season

fuerte strong

gachas malaguenas potato pancakes, from Malaga

a la gallega from Galicia

galletas biscuits, often served with coffee at breakfast-time, they are usually fairly thin and crisp, with a very mild spice flavouring

gallina chicken, usually a rather tough hen, best for stewing; *en pepitoria*, casseroled with onions, garlic, wine and herbs and finished with almonds and hard-boiled egg; *puchero de gallina*, stuffedwith herbs and breadcrumbs, and casseroled in stock; *en pebre*, in garlic sauce

gambas prawns; *a la plancha*, cooked on a hot plate in their shells, with oil, lemon juice and garlic

ganso goose; *relleno de castañas*, stuffed with chestnuts

garbanzos chick peas

garneo piper fish; member of the gurnard family

gazpacho a vegetable soup served iced; there are many variations: to a base of breadcrumbs, garlic, olive oil, wine vinegar are added some or all of the following – tomatoes, cucumber, green and red peppers, onions; in Catalonia pine kernels or hazlenuts are added; in Andalucia almonds; *gazpacho blanco* is made with white and green ingredients, and garnished with grapes

giraboix a vegetable stew, from Alicante

girasol sunflower

granada pomegranate

grañon a wheat-based vegetable stew, from Allicante

al gratén *au gratin*

greixera one of the traditional meat and vegetable stews of Spain, named after the pot in which it is cooked, from the Balearics

grosellas gooseberiies

guindilla chili

guisado/a(s) stew, stewed

guisantes peas; *secos*, dried peas; *menestra de guisantes*, stewed with ham, chicken and artichokes

habas broad beans, also known as *faves*; *a la Catalana*, with *butifarra negra*, spring onions, parsley and mint; *de vitoria*, with *chorizo*, ham and fat bacon; *a la asturiana*, with potatoes, carrots, ham and white wine; *cazuela a la granadina*, casseroled with onions, tomatoes, artichokes and fried bread in crumbs; eggs are broken into it to finish

harina flour

helado ice-cream; *copa helada*, ice-cream sundae; *un barquillo*, ice-cream cone

hierbabuena mint

higado liver; *frito*, fried with oil and garlic, sometimes with sherry added; *a la asturiana*, casseroled with onions, tomatoes and wine, and finished with almonds and garlic pounded together, from Asturias

higos figs

hinojo fennel; *marino*, samphire

hojaldre flaky pastry

hojas leaves (e.g. of cabbage); *de viña*, vine leaves

hongo mushroom, cep

horchata (de chufas) a sweet drink made from the milk of ground tiger nuts or *chufas*

horgaza a loaf of bread (but if you are shopping it will be sufficient to ask for *pan*)

European Menu Guide

hornazo a pastry filled with *chorizo*, meat and hard-boiled eggs, made on the Monday following Easter Monday, from Old Castile

al horno baked

hueso bone, stone (of cherry)

huesos de santo 'saint's bones', sweet bone-shaped or cylindrical cakes, stuffed with a filling of egg yolks and sugar

huevas fish roes

huevo(s) egg(s); *duro*, hard-boiled; *revuelto*, scrambled; *pasado por agua*, soft boiled; *escalfado*, poached; *al plato* or *frito*, fried; *a la extremeña*, eggs baked in a tomato sauce with potatoes, *chorizo* and ham; *a la flamenca*, eggs baked in a ham and tomato sauce with *chorizo*, asparagus tips and red pepper; *relleno*, stuffed with mayonnaise, and sometimes with tuna, or anchovies; *al nido*, in a hollowed-out roll; *a la alicantina*, in hollowed-out potatoes in prawn sauce; *a la santanderina*, with peas and asparagus; *a la valenciana*, on a paella base; *a la riojana*, with *chorizo*, tomatoes and peppers

inglés English; *pudding inglés*, plum pudding; *cake inglés*, plum cake, fruit cake

intxausalsa sweet cream of walnuts, a Basque recipe

jabalí wild boar

jamón ham; *serrano*, eaten raw in thin slices, this is a great delicacy, the best comes from the province of Huelva, where it is cured in the cold, dry mountain air; *de York*, cooked ham in the English-style

al jerez in a sherry sauce

judías beans; *verdes*, French beans; *blancas*, haricot beans; *blancas a lo tío Lucas*, "Uncle Lucas' beans, cooked with onions, garlic, paprika, cumin and parsley, from madrid; *con tomate*, with tomatoes

jugo juice; *en su jugo*, (cooked) in its own juices

jurel scad or horse mackerel

kokotxas the front part, the mouth and throat, of the hake; *a la donostiarra*, in garlic, parsley and oil

lacón con grelos a traditional Galician dish, of *lacón*, the upper part of the front legs of the pig, and *grelos*, a kind of cabbage, with beans and *chorizo*

lamprea lamprey

langosta spiny lobster; *a la catalana*, with onions, garlic, saffron, paprika, chocolate, nutmeg and brandy; *extremeña*, cooked with onions, garlic and herbs, and served with a creamy sauce; *a la barcelonesa*. sautéd with chicken pieces and baked with a tomato and almond sauce

langostino large prawn

lata tin; *atún de lata*, tinned tuna

laurel bay leaf

leche milk; *frita*, fried squares of custard

lechuga lettuce

lechecillas de ternera calves' sweetbreads

legumbres, verduras vegetables

lengua(s) tongue; *a la aragonesa*, cooked with peppers, carrots, onion, tomatoes, garlic and chocolate

lenguado sole; *en filete*, fillets

lentejas lentils; *y anchoas*, brown lentils with anchovies; *zamoranas*, with black puddins, onions, garlic and paprika

liebre hare; *guiso de liebre con salsa de sangre*, stewed in its blood; *en su salsa*, marinated in white wine, then cooked with its liver in red wine and vegetables

limón lemon

llebre amb xocolata hare in chocolate sauce, a Catalan dish

llenguado alacanti sole Alicante-style; fried, with a sauce of orange juice, almonds and pine kernels

lisa grey mullet

lomo loin; frequently means pork loin, *lomo de cerdo*, a very popular cut of meat in Spain often found simply fried in oil

lomo de cerdo fillet of pork; *a la aragonesa*, with onions, tomatoes, garlic and red wine; *a la catalana*, with fried haricot beans; *almendrado*, baked with an almond stuffing

longaniza sausages of the *sobresada* type, sold in strings, for cooking only

lubina bass; *asturiana*, baked with wine and mussels

maccarones macaroni

macedonia de frutas fruit salad

magdalenas the Spanish version of *madeleines* (small, round sponge cakes)

magras cubes of lean pork or raw smoked ham in a tomato sauce

European Menu Guide

mahón firm cow's milk cheese with a dark rind, from Mahón in Menorca

mahonesa/mayonesa mayonnaise; a very popular dressing for cold vegetables, meat and fish, often used in *tapas*

malvices a dish of the Rioja regions of tiny birds fried whole

manchego firm, white, mature sheep'-milk cheese with a distinctive hard, dark rind with ridged sides, the most widely-known of Spain's cheeses, mainly produced in Castile

manos de cerdo pig's trotters; often used in thick soups and stews such as *cocido*; *empanadas*, dipped in egg and breadcrumbs and fried

manteca lard

mantecados shortcakes made with lard

mantequilla butter

manzana(s) apple(s); *asadas*, baked apples

maravillas 'little wonders'. little fried cakes

a la marinera 'fisherman's-style'. with white wine, onions, garlic and parsley

mariscos shellfish

marmitako mackerel stew with potatoes and peppers, a Basque recipe

marzapan marzipan; a speciality of Toledo sold in little cakes

masa dough

matanza a pig-killing; often the occasion for a special meal, which will be called *de matanza*

medallones medallions

filete filler (of meat, fish)

mejillones mussels

mejorana marjoram

mel i mató cottage cheese with honey, from Catalonia

merluza hake; *al hinojo*, with fennel; *a la gallega*, poached, served with potatoes and onions; *koskera*, fried and topped with asparagus and a hard-boiled egg, from Old Castile; *rebozada*, fried in batter, *con pistillo*, baked with cheese and breadcrumbs, and served with *pistillo*, a sauce of onions, red peppers, tomatoes, capers and hard-boiled egg yolk; *a la romana*, fried in batter

mermelada jam

mero grouper fish; *a la vizcaína*, in a hot pepper sauce, a

Basque recipe; *a la valenciana*, dipped in seasoned flour and fried, with garlic and saffron; *al jerez*, baked in olive oil, sherry and almonds

migas literally 'crumbs', cubes of bread fried in spiced oil, from Andalucia; *canas*, bread, *chorizo* and bacon baked in milk and spices, garnished with black grapes, a Castilian recipe

mixto/a(s) mixed

mojete salad of baked red peppers in vinaigrette

molde mould

mollejas lamb's sweetbreads

montsec distinctive goat's-milk cheese matured in a cave, giving a creamy cheese with a mildewed rind, from Catalonia

moraga de sardinas fresh sardines with white wine, parsley and garlic

moras mulberries

morcilla a smoked blood sausage of pig's blood, fat, onions and spices, with a strong smoky flavour, used in *fabada*; *morcilla dulce* is sweet and spicy, from Asturias

morros cheek; *de ternera a la vizcaína*, calf's cheek in red peppers and onions, a Basque dish

mortéruelo a spicy liver paté from Castile

mostaza mustard

motllo d'alberginies a form of timbale of aubergines, from Mallorca

nabo turnip; *con jamón*, cooked with serrano ham

naranja orange

nata cream

natillas custard flavoured with lemon and cinnamon

neules a type of *crêpe* eaten at Christmas, a Catalan recipe

al nido in a nest

nuez, nueces nut, nuts; *moscada*, nutmeg

oblada the saddled bream. Alan Davidson quotes a recipe from the Balearics, *oblada con verdura*, in which the fish is baked with chard, raisins and white wine, and served with sliced, fried potatoes

oliaigua soup of olive oil, garlic, parsley, salt and water, eaten with bread, from Menorca; *amb tomàquets*, with tomato; *amb col*, with cabbage

European Menu Guide

olla podrida 'rotten pot', a traditional name for the stew that is now known as *cocido madrileño*

oporto port

orégano wild marjoram

ostras oysters

paella a rice dish, of seafood (may include prawns, mussels, squid, lobster, white fish), meat (usually chicken, or rabbit or pork), usually coloured with saffron, with vegetables such as peas, tomatoes, red peppers, cooked and served in a round flat pan, a *paëllera*, garnished with lemon wedges; the most well-known recipe comes from Valencia

palitos 'little sticks'; *de queso*, cheese straws

palometa a fish of the carangidae family, with firm white flesh

palometón fish of the carangidae family, with a firm flesh, like tuna-fish

pan bread; *integral*, brown; *rallados*, breadcrumbs

pan con tomate bread rubbed with fresh tomatoes, oil, garlic and salt often topped with *jamón serrano*; variations include chopped nuts sprinkled on buttered bread, toast topped with tomatoes, oil and blood sausage, and rolls filled with grilled red peppers, chopped onion and some chopped sausage or *tortilla*, from Catalonia

pan dulce 'sweet bread', made with dried and candied fruits

panchineta puff pastry tart with almond topping, a Basque recipe

panellets petits fours made from almond paste, often made for All Saints Day, from Catalonia

pantortillas puff pastry pancakes flavoured with *anís*, served cold

paprika paprika, a very popular seasoning

a la parrilla grilled

pargo sea bream; *encebollado*, the fish is baked whole on a bed of chopped tomatoes, onions, walnuts and peppers

pasas raisins; *malagueñas*, from Malaga, the best – the fattest and juiciest

Pascua Easter; *cordero pascual*, Easter lamb

pastel(-eles) cake(s), pastries, both sweet and savoury; *de pescado*, fish pie, a Galician recipe, has almonds, garlic, onions and tomatoes, all topped with mashed potato; *de* *murcia*, a tart filled with chorizo, veal, hard-boiled eggs and brains

pastis dolç de peix 'sweet fish cake', filled with fried eels, spinach, onion, garlic, egg, butter and sugar, from the Balearics

pastissets fullats small, stuffed puff pastries from Menorca; *amb colomins*, with pastries; *amb gambes*, with prawns

patatas potatoes; *puré de patatas*, potato purée; *fritas*, chips; *rellenas*, peeled, boiled and baked with a stuffing which usually contains meat; *asadas*, roast; *en ajo pollo*, cooked with a mixture of bread, almonds, garlic and parsley pounded together; *castellanas*, fried with onion, garlic and paprika, and then cooked slowly in liquid; *a la riojana*, with *chorizo*

pato duck; *al estilo de Ribadeo*, with oranges, turnips, carrots, chestnuts, anis and white wine; *a la sevillana*, casseroled, and served in a sauce of red peppers, garlic and tomatoes, and garnished with olives, oranges and peppers

pavo turkey

pechuga(s) de pollo chicken breast(s)

pepino cucumber

pepitoria fricassée

pera pear

perdins amb col partridges stuffed with cabbage, tomato, minced pork and *chorizo*, and seasoning, from Catalonia

perdiz(-ices) partridge(s); *a la catalana*, with herbs and lemon; *asturiana*, with *tocino*, onions, herbs and cider; *a la torera*, with ham, anchovies, tomatoes and green peppers; *a la toledana*, with potatoes and white wine; *estofadas*, with onions, garlic, mushrooms, red wine and chocolate; *escabechadas*, cooked in stock with wine and vinegar and then soused in oil and vinegar until cold

perejil parsley

pescado(s) fish; *a la sal*, a large fish baked whole in a shell of rock salt, this preserves the moisture and flavour, served with hollandaise sauce and boiled potatoes; *fritos*, a dish of mixed fish, dipped in flour and fried in oil, very common in restaurants and roadside bars; *ventas* in Andalucia; *en escabeche*, marinated in garlic, saffron, lemon and ginger

European Menu Guide

pescadilla small hake

pescados, mariscos fish, shellfish dishes

pessigolles de xocolata chocolate meringues, a Catalan recipe

pestiños sweet fritters, flavoured with sesame and anis seeds and honey

pez de limón amberjack fish; Alan Davidson quotes a recipe from the Balearics, *Sirviola con salsa*, in which the fish is served with a sauce of carrots, pimentos, garlic and tomatoes – slices of bread dipped in milk, then in beated egg and fried are served with the dish

pez piloto pilot fish; often cooked like mackerel

picada used in Catalan cooking for finishing sauces and soups, a hot garlicky paste based not on flour but on ground almonds or hazelnuts

picadillo a minced dish; *de cerdo*, minced pork fried in lard with marjoram, paprika and seasonings

pichón(-ones) pigeons

picon creamy blue cheese wrapped in chestnut leaves, made from a mixture of sheep's, goat's, and cow's milk, from the Picos de Europa

pierna leg; *de cordero*, leg of lamb; *sin hueso*, boned leg

pilotes de peix fish balls poached in stock, from the Balearics

pimentón dried, powdered red pepper; *picante* is cayenne, *dulce* is paprika

pimiento(s) sweet pepper(s); *rojos/morrones*, red; *verdes*, green; there are two types, one large and with a rounded end, the other longer and thinner with a pointed end; *rellenos*, the stuffings are either rice – or breadcrumb-based, with meat and herbs

piña pineapple

pinchitos little kebabs, often served as *tapas*

piñones pine kernels

piparrada pipérade, peppers, onions and tomatoes cooked with beaten eggs, a Basque recipe

piriñaca a salad of chopped tomatoes, onions, green peppers and garlic dressed in oil and vinegar; also used as a sauce in which to bake bream, *con besugo asado cau piriñaca*

pisto a stew of tomatoes, courgetes, onions and peppers, rather like *ratatouille*; *manchego*, from La Mancha

a la plancha cooked on an oiled hot plate: this is used for everything from eggs to fish and steaks

plátano banana

platillo d'anyell à la catalana fricassée of lamb with *sofregit* or *sofrito* of onions, tomatoes and garlic, with peas, potatoes and shallots, finished with a hot, garlicky *picada*, from Catalonia

pochas riojanas stew made from a type of haricot bean which is not dried, with *chorizo*, from the Rioja region

pollo chicken; the male bird, best for roasting; *asado*, roast; *frito*, fried; *a la manchega*, casseroled with carrots, cabbage, turnips and olives, from La Mancha; *menestra de pollo*, casseroled with peas, potatoes, asparagus, artichokes and ham

polvorones a type of powdery shortbread, of flour, sugar, lard and cinnamon, originating from Andalusia

postre dessert

potaje thick soup; *de berros*, watercress soup with puréed beans or chick peas; *canariense*, a thick soup of chick peas and mixed vegetables, spiced with paprika and cumin, from the Canary Islands

pote gallego the Galician version of the traditional stew of meat and vegetables which is usually served in two or three courses, named after the *pote* or pot in which it is cooked

primavera spring

puchero a traditional stew of meat and vegetables, named after the *puchero* or pot in which it is cooked

puerro leek

pulpo octopus; *guisado*, casseroled with a sweet red pepper, paprika, cayenne, fennel and white wine, from Catalonia

punta tip (e.g. of asparagus)

puntillitas tiny inkfish, fried in batter, from Andalucia

puré purée

quemado/a(s) burnt

quesada a pastry case filled with coconut, eggs and sugar, from the Basque country

queso cheese; Spain's cheeses are not so varied as those of

European Menu Guide

France, but you can find some interesting speciality cheeses, expecially in the north; *manchego* is probably the most well-known cheese, it is separately listed under 'm', and a number of other cheeses can be found listed alphabetically; *rallado*, grated; *de la serena*, yellow cheese with yellow rind made from merino sheep's milk, from La Serena in Extremadura; *de la selva*, creamy yellow cheese, from Galicia; *de los ibores*, goat's-milk cheese, produced either oiled, or coated in paprika, or natural, from Extremadura; *de cabra*, goat's milk cheese; *de bola*, cow's milk cheese, resembling Edam

quisquilla prawn

rábano picante horseradish

rascasio rockfish

raspallón a member of the bream family

(bizcochos) rellenos de vergara pastries filled with an egg yolk and sugar mixture, a Basque speciality

rabo de toro oxtail stew

rape angler fish; *a la Costa Brava*, with peas, red peppers, mussels, saffron, garlic and white wine; *con patatas*, with potatoes, tomatoes and red peppers; *al horno*, baked with a sauce of tomatoes, almonds, peanuts and breadcrumbs, from Malaga

raviolis Catalan pastries filled with *cabello de angel* conserve

raya skate; *en pimentón*, with paprika; *con salsa de mantequilla negra*, with black butter

rebozos zamoranos small lemon flavoured cakes, from Zamora

relleno/a(s) stuffed

remojón salad of cod, seville oranges, onions, hard boiled eggs and olives, from Andalucia

remolacha beetroot

revuelto/a(s) scrambled

roales/revoles de menorca small croquettes of fish, seafood, or spinach, from Menorca

rodajas strips

romesco the classic Catalan sauce of hot red peppers, garlic, almonds, and paprika, for meat and fish – the equivalent of the French *rouille*

riñoes kidneys; *riñonada*, a dish of lamb's kidneys and sweetbreads; *al jerez*, fried and then served with a sauce of sherry and tomato paste

rodaballo turbot; *marinera*, poached, with a sauce of white wine, brandy, tomato purée and mussels

romero rosemary

ron rum

ropa vieja 'old clothers', a traditional stew of beef with onions, peppers, aubergines and tomatoes

rosquillas a type of doughnut, ring-shaped, often flavoured with anis seeds; *de San Isidro*, named after Madrid's patron saint, and flavoured with a glass of 'Anis del Mono,' a polular sweet *anis* liqueur

rubio streaked gurnard fish; one of the tastiest of this family

sal salt

a la sal a method of cooking fish inside a shell of salt, retaining all the juices of the fish

salchichas sausages

salchichón a salami-like sausage, of pork, pork fat and white peppercorns, usually eaten raq as a *tapa*

salmón salmon; *ahumado*, smoked salmon; *con aceitunas*, baked with green olives, seasoning and oil and vinegar, garnished with hard-boiled eggs

salmonete red mullet; *a la parrilla*, marinaded in olive oil, salt and lemon juice, then grilled; *envueltos*, wrapped in bacon rashers and charcoal grilled

salmorejo a thick gazpacho, without the peppers or tomatoes, from Cordoba

salpiquet de mongetes casserole of haricot beans, a Catalan dish

salsa sauce; *de mojo*, 'red sauce' of garlic, paprika, cumin, thyme, oil and vinegar served with potatoes as a *tapa*, from the Canary Islands; *de piñones*, of pine kernels, cumin and egg yolks, from Catalonia; *picante*, onion, garlic and cayenne with oil and vinegar, for meat and fish; *verde*, 'green sauce', of oil, garlic and parsley, and sometimes peas, served with eel or hake; *española*, 'Spanish sauce', the classic brown sauce; *besamel*, béchamel; *bearnesa*, béarnaise; *de almendras*, almond sauce, with almonds and hard-boiled egg yolks

salteado/a(s) sautéed

salvia sage

samfaina a sauce of onion, aubergine, courgettes, ham, peppers and tomatoes, for chicked and pork, from Catalonia

San Pedro John Dory or St Peter fish

sancocho canario boiled fish and potatoes in a chilli sauce, from the Canary Islands

sandía watermelon

sangre blood

sangría a refreshing drink of red wine, mixed with brandy and lemonade, very often served up to tourists

sardinas sardines; often served quickly fried, *fritas*; *a la santanderina*, fried, then cooked in a tomato, onion and garlic sauce, from Santander; *rebozadas*, fried in batter; salted sardines can be seen in grocers everywhere, packed in a wheel shape in wooden barrels; *salpimenteadas*, salted overnight, then grilled with green peppers and chili peppers; *a la teja*, cooked on an earthenware roof tile, in a traditional way

sargo a member of the bream family

secco dry

sepia cuttlefish

sequillos lemon flavoured hazelnut biscuits

servilleta creamy cheese 80% goat's milk, 20% cow's milk, shaped in a napkin, hence its name, from Valencia

sesos brains; often served fried, *fritos*, or in a *tortilla*

setas field mushrooms

sidra cider

sobresada a large orange-coloured sausage made of pork, pork tripe, paprika, cayenne and salt, soft enough to spread on bread, often eaten at breakfast, from Mallorca

sofrito chopped onions and tomatoes fried together, sometimes with garlic and peppers – a basic sauce for many recipes; *ibicenco*, casseroled lamb, chicken and *sobresadas*, spiced with cumin, saffron and garlic, from Ibizia

solomillo sirloin

sopa soup; *de almendras*, a smooth soup of almonds, garlic, oil and vinegar, garnished with grapes, served cold; *de galets*, with pork meatballs and pasta shells ('galets' in

Catalonia); *de vainas*, green bean soup garnished with olives and bread slices topped with cheese, a Basque recipe; *de ajo*, garlic soup, often garnished with peppers, or an egg is beaten in before serving; *escaldada*, a vegetable soup of lentils with a variety of vegetables, and a little *sobresada* and *tocino*, poured onto a slice of brown bread in each bowl, from Mallorca; *de lentejas*, lentil soup, with peppers, tomatoes and carrots, from Madrid; *de picadillo*, a clear soup based on meat stock, garnished with chopped ham and hard-boiled egg, from Andalucia; *de peix*, fish soup, from Mallorca; *al cuarto de hora* (made in) 'a quarter of an hour' soup, of ham, hard-boiled eggs, clams, onions, garlic, parsley and bread; *de aragón*, a slice of toast, covered with stock and topped with sieved calf's liver and grated cheese

sopa d'ametlles a sweet almond soup served hot as a dessert, garnished with 'croûtons' of cake, from the Balearics

sorbete sorbet

suquet de pescado a fish stew, with tomatoes and garlic, from Catalonia

suquillo a fish stew

suspiros d monja 'nun's sighs', egg whites poached in milk, with a cinnamon sauce – the equivalent of *oeufs à la neige*

tallo stalk, stem (of chard)

talos a form of *tortilla* made with maize flour and water, baked and then fried, from the Basque country

tapas to be found in every bar in every city from midday onwards: these are tiny portions of hot and cold dishes served with a little bread and a glass of beer, sherry or wine, they range from a few olives or some slices of *chorizo* to the ubiquitous *tortilla* and Russian salad, and small portions of stews, or fresh seafood. An excellent way to discover Spanish cooking and if you move from one bar to another between 12 and 3, you won't need any lunch

tarta tart; *de puentedeume*, filled with almonds, egg yolks and sugar; *helada*, ice-cream gateau

a la teja cooked on a hot earthenware roof tile, a traditional method of cooking

tenca tench

European Menu Guide

ternera veal; *con alcachofas a la cordobesa*, with artichokes and Montilla; *en adobo*, marinated in wine; *a la riojana*, veal steaks fried with green peppers

ternasco young lamb

tetilla mild yellow cow's-milk cheese with a conical shape, from Galicia

tocinillo de almendra almond cake

tocino salted pork fat; *tocino de cielo*, a dessert made from egg yolks, sugar and vanilla, like a more solid version of caramel custard

tomate(s) tomato(es); *rellenos de alicante*, stuffed with spinach, and topped with orange juice and minced almonds

tomillo thyme

toronja grapefruit

torrades (de Santa Teresa) a Catalan version of *torrijas*

torrijas slices of bread soaked in milk, dipped in egg and deep fried, then soaked in syrup

torta tart; *tortas de aceite*, 'oil cakes', crisp, sweet biscuits

tortilla omelette; usually made of potatoes (with optional onions or *chorizo*) and served in wedges from a round cake an inch or more thick, often eaten as a *tapa* or in a *bocadillo*; *al sacromonte*, of lamb's brains and sweetbreads, from the Gypsy quarter of Granada; *francesa*, french omelette; *a la magra*, with strips of pork fillet; *de butifarra y mongetes*, with bufifarra and haricot beans which have been boiled and then fried; *al carreña*, with asparagus, ham and *chorizo*; *murciana*, with red peppers and tomatoes; *riojana* with ham, *chorizo* and peppers

tostada toast; either sliced bread or a crusty roll split in half

tourín a Catalan soup, into which egg yolks are stirred, topped with fried bread

trigo wheat; *sarraceno*, buckwheat

trinxat fried potato and cabbage, from Catalonia

tronchon volcano-shaped mild flavoured cheese from wither sheep's or goat's milk or both, from the Maestrago region, near Teruel

turcha(s) trout; *de león*, grilled – the trout of this region are very good, and are often cooked locally over a wood fire on a wire grid; *rellenas*, stuffed; *truchas canarias*, spiced doughnuts, from the Canary Islands; *a la montañesa*, in white wine with onions and bay leaves

trufa truffle

tumbet onions, potatoes, courgettes, peppers baked with tomato sauce and beated egg, from the Balearics

turrón nougat, a Christmas treat sold in blocks or round cakes; Alicante *turrón* comes in a number of flavours and shapes

urta sea bream, popular baked whole in the restaurants of the provinces of Seville and Cadiz

uvas grapes

vaca cow, beef; *asada de vaca*, pot-roasted beef

al vapor steamed

vega sauco mature sheep's-milk cheese, from Zamora

venado venison

verduras vegetables

vieiras scallops; *guisadas* or *peregrinas*, the shells are stuffed and baked with scallop flesh, garlic, parsley and onions, topped with breadcrumbs, a speciality of Santiago de Compostela

vinagre vinegar; wine vinegar is always used

vino wine; *blanco*, white; *tinto*, red; *rosado*, rosé; *dulce*, sweet; *seco*, dry; *de mesa*, table wine

xató a form of *salad niçoise*, of *bacalao*, tuna, olives, tomatoes, anchovies, garlic, almonds and vinaigrette, a Catalan dish eaten before Lent begins

xuxos de girona cream-filled *beignets*

yemas sweets made from egg yolks and sugar, a Castilian speciality

zanahorias carrots

zarzuela de mariscos/pescado literally 'a musical comedy', this is a mixture of shellfish and white fish with saffron, garlic and white wine

zumo de fruta fruit juice

zurrukutuna salt cold soup with green peppers, with eggs poached in it just before serving, a Basque recipe